JAVA

JAVA BASICS FOR BEGINNERS

Andy Vickler

Table of Contents

v

Introduction

This book contains proven steps and strategies on how to learn the basics of Java. Java is a comparatively tough language to learn because it is not scripted but compiled. You need a Java Development Kit and a compiler to create projects, save files, and run codes.

I have written this book in a way that explains the basics of Java programming. You will be introduced to the installation process of the Java Development Kit and the compilers. There are many compilers available in the market. You can use one of your choice and create Java codes. As classes are inherent in Java, you should make sure that the file names you are creating are in line with the names of the classes. Otherwise, you will see an error in the compiler.

This book contains an introduction to Java syntax, variables, conditionals, loops, and object-oriented programming. I recommend that you should keep an editor and compiler ready to write and test the codes that you learn from the book. You can introduce some changes to the code and test them again to see whether they work or not.

Java is a bit different from other programming languages like Python because of its different names for lists, arrays, and dictionaries. Therefore, if you get yourself acquainted with the vocabulary, you will find it easy to navigate through the codes. For example, HashMap is similar to dictionaries in other programming languages. ArrayLists and LinkedLists work like normal lists in other programming languages.

You don't have to be an expert in programming to start this book. Anyone who has an interest in coding can buy this book and understand the ins and outs of Java programming. I have included a code sample for each section of the book so that you can understand how a code works whenever you see that in the book. Even each method in the book is explained with a proper example.

Therefore, the best way is to read the book and practice it as well at the same time. Use the codes, edit them, and compile them to see what results you can produce. Customize the codes so that you can learn how to write your own codes. Java, over the past years, managed to retain its popularity among programmers. And it is likely to gain more in the future.

Chapter One

Java Installation

Java falls into the category of one of the most influential and most used programming languages. The journey of Java began in 1990 when an American company, which was, at that point, in the quest to lead the revolution in the computer industry, opted to collect the top engineers and assign them the task to develop a product that would ultimately make them a key player in the emerging world of the internet. Among the engineers was Hames Arthur Gosling. James was a Canadian computer scientist who is now well-known as the father of Java.

The first version of Java got its release in 1996. A team named the Green team worked on the prototype language, which was then known as Oak. It had a working demo which is an interactive handheld home-entertainment controller, also known as the Star.

Java is considered a portable language, and Java can run on any operating system. It is a high-end programming language that allows developers to write programs that can exist independent of any working operating system like a computer. Mostly high-level programming languages are way easier to compose and maintain. However, the code needs to be translated by a compiler. It should be interpreted in a machine language in order to be executed because it is the machine language that a computer understands.

You will need a Java Virtual Machine(JVM) for Java so that Java can be run on a computer. A JVM is required for the execution of different Java programs that you create. This platform will convert the code of Java into a machine language that the computer understands. After the conversion, it will execute the same.

The compile source code of other high-level programming languages is compiled directly into the machine code that is specifically designed to run on a microprocessor operating system like UNIX or Windows. JVM, on the other hand, mimics the Java processor and makes it possible for Java programs to be interpreted as a sequence of actions on a processor no matter what the operating system is.

The Development Environment

When you make up your mind to start working in Java, you need a couple of things properly installed on your operating system. Here is the rundown of the requirements you need. First of all, you need Java support on your operating system. You also need an integrated development environment (IDE), which is an application to write code to compile and execute.

The recommended IDE is IntelliJ IDE. You can browse their website to get the community edition for free. You also can choose a highly popular IDE, namely Eclipse, which you can get for free. The third version of IDE is called NetBeans.

Gradle is a built-in tool that is used for the organization of projects so that you can easily handle certain dependencies. It can facilitate your work as your projects become bigger. Another version Git is a versioning system that you may use to get the sources for this book.

How To Install

You have got your computer system. First of all, you have to get a JDK and then install it right away on your computer system. You will need a stable internet connection to open it and install it from the website.

When it has been opened, you need to scroll down to the Downloads section. Now click the Java SE link. Look out for the latest version of Java on the official website of Oracle. Now click the Download JDK button, and you will be redirected to a new page.

JDK is available for a couple of operating systems. You may download the one that matches yours. You should accept the license agreement before you are allowed to download the version of JDK you need. You can read the agreement if you want to get yourself familiar with the contents before you start. If we summarize it in simple words, the agreement tells you that the user will be allowed to use Java if you do not have any planning to modify the original components. It tells you that you will be responsible for its usage, so if you use the same to either write or execute its dangerous applications, you will be held legally responsible.

If you want to declare the JAVA_HOME environment variable on Windows, you must open the dialog box to set up the variables of the system. On the Windows operating system, you need to hit the Start button. Inside the menu section, you will find a search box. Now type in the word environment. The exact option, namely Environment, will show up for clicking. Click the button. There will be another dialog box, split up into two sections called system variables and user variables.

After you have defined the JAVA_HOME variable, you have to add executables to the path of the system. This will be done by formally editing the Path variable. All you need is to select the variable from the list of System Variables and then hit the Edit button. You can see each section of the Path variable onto a different line so that you may add a different line.

Using Shell

The Java Shell tool or JShell is a really interactive tool to learn the ins and outs of Java programming and prototyping Java code, which means that you can write the code and also execute it in the same console. You don't have to save it first and then compile it into bytecode to run it, and after that, get it interpreted by the operating system as a line of instructions for execution. JShell is a bit late to the world of Java as Scripting languages such as Node and Python have already introduced similar kinds of utilities a couple of years ago. JVM languages like Clojure, Scala, and Groovy have also adopted it a while ago. However, as the saying goes, it is better late than never. Therefore, even the late coming has been accepted.

JShell is REPL, which means Read-Eval-Print Loop. It tends to evaluate the declarations, the statements, and the expressions as you enter them, and then it shows the results fast. It is quite practical to try out fresh ideas and techniques faster without the need to have a full development environment or a complete text for the code to be executed.

JShell is like a standard component of JDK and is quite executable to begin. It rests in the bin directory that is located in the JDK installation directory. It means that you just have to open up a terminal like a command prompt in Windows and then type jshell as the command. You will see something like the following.

```
C:\Users\saifia computers>jshell
|  Welcome to JShell -- Version 16.0.1
|  For an introduction type: /help intro
jshell>
```

You can then go ahead and enter /help to view a list of actions and commands in jshell. See the following list here.

```
jshell> /help
|  Type a Java language expression,
statement, or declaration.
|  Or type one of the following commands:
|  /list [<name or id>|-all|-start]
|       list the source you have typed
|  /edit <name or id>
|        edit a source entry
|  /drop <name or id>
```

7

```
|        delete a source entry
|   /save [-all|-history|-start] <file>
|        Save snippet source to a file
|   /open <file>
|        open a file as source input
|   /vars [<name or id>|-all|-start]
|        list the declared variables and
their values
|   /methods [<name or id>|-all|-start]
|        list the declared methods and their
signatures
|   /types [<name or id>|-all|-start]
|        list the type declarations
|   /imports
|        list the imported items
|   /exit [<integer-expression-snippet>]
|        exit the jshell tool
```

The list is long. I have only added the first few items from the list to give you an overview of how it looks and what you will find in there. If you want to see what Jshell is currently doing, type in the – v command and see how it works. You can assign values in Java to variables, which are sequences of different characters. I will now create a variable of type integer and then assign it a value of 55. See how to do that.

```
jshell> int a=55
a ==> 55

jshell>
```

You can see that the command was successfully executed, and a value was assigned to the variable. Line a ==>55 lets us know that the value 5 has been assigned to the variable that you have just

8

created. You can declare as many variables as you want. I will now create another variable with a different value.

```
jshell> int x=556
x ==> 556

jshell>
```

As long as you do not close the jshell session, the variables will exist, and their values will remain intact. We can use them further on. Now let us add the two variables and see the output. I will use the + operator to get the sum of the two variables in the jshell. The process is the same as it is in plain mathematics. See the following piece of code.

```
jshell> int a=55
a ==> 55

jshell> int x=556
x ==> 556

jshell> a + x
$4 ==> 611

jshell>
```

I have added two variables, but I have not stored the result of the two in a third variable. That's why jshell has created a scratch variable for storing the result of the two and printing the same inside the log. However, that variable can never be used in the later statements because it lacks a name. Now everything seems fine. You can create variables and execute operations perfectly.

Anything that you can write in Java can also be written in jshell and then executed as well.

The basic building blocks of Java are known as classes. These are pieces of code that are modeled on real-world objects as well as events. Java classes contain different types of members; those that are modeled to states are known as class variables, and those that are modeled on behavior are called methods. Class variables are also known as properties and fields. Now I will declare the first string variable in the following section.

```
jshell> String msg = "I am starting to learn
Java development."
msg ==> "I am starting to learn Java
development."

jshell>
```

I have declared a variable of String type and then named it as msg. You can name it whatever you like. The String class carries several methods that you may call for text modification purposes. I will call one method to turn the piece of text into upper case in the next example.

```
jshell> String msg = "I am starting to learn
Java development."
msg ==> "I am starting to learn Java
development."

jshell> msg.toUpperCase()
$7 ==> "I AM STARTING TO LEARN JAVA
DEVELOPMENT."
```

```
jshell>
```

The final statement is known as the String method. It has turned the piece of text into uppercase. Let us see what happens when you type in something that is not recognized by Java.

```
jshell> msg.toMultiverse()
|  Error:
|  cannot find symbol
|    symbol:   method toMultiverse()
|  msg.toMultiverse()
|  ^--------------^

jshell>
```

JShell will tell you in clear words that it does not recognize the command. It will not recognize plain text either. You can create more methods as well.

```
jshell> String creatingHello(String x){
   ...>      return "Hello " + x;
   ...> }
|  created method creatingHello(String)

jshell> creatingHello(msg)
$9 ==> "Hello I am starting to learn Java
development."

jshell>
```

If you need to see the variables that you already have declared in the JShell play session, you may do so by the execution of the vars command. The command will display a list of all the variables that I have just created in the shell.

```
jshell> /vars
|    int i = 42
|    int a = 55
|    int x = 556
|    int $4 = 611
|    String text = "I am starting to learn
Java development."
|    String msg = "I am starting to learn
Java development."
|    String $7 = "I AM STARTING TO LEARN
JAVA DEVELOPMENT."
|    String $9 = "Hello, I am starting to
learn Java development."

jshell>
```

Java Fundamental Building Blocks

If you want to be an expert coder, you need to have a good grasp of what happens inside Java. What are the building blocks, and how have those building blocks been connected with each other? You need to be well-versed in the building blocks of the Java ecosystem. The core of the ecosystem is classes. Classes are the most important because they represent templates for objects that make up different types of applications. A class groups different methods and fields. When you create an object, the values of all the fields define what the state of an object is. It also describes the behavior of methods.

The Java object models a real-world object. If you choose to model a bike in Java, you will have to define different fields that will describe the bike. The fields can be the model of the car, the make of the car, the price of the car, the color of the car, the engine power of the car, the type of the car, and the seating capacity of the car. It will define its functions like speeding and braking as well.

You need to describe all types of objects in files and add to them the .java extension. You can organize object types in the form of packages. A package in Java is a logical collection of different types. Some of these types are completely visible out of the package, and some are not based on the scope. A package is like a hierarchy of directories, and the Java object types are the last.

The name of the packages must be unique, and their name should also follow a set template. In order to ensure meaning and unicity, you need to start the name with the Internet Domain name of your organization in reverse order. Then you need to add different types of grouping criteria. Each package can contain a file named package-info.java that will contain the package declaration, the annotations, the comments, and Javadoc tags. The comments are then exported to Javadoc for the package. The package file needs to rest in the last directory inside the package.

The files that carry *.java extension have the object types definitions and are compiled in the form of files that have *.class, organized as per the package structure, and then packaged into multiple JARs.

The code that rests inside a package spans more than one JARs, which means that if you have more than one subproject in the project, you will have the name of the same package multiple times. Also, it will contain different classes. A Java library makes use of multiple libraries. In order to be run, it needs all the dependencies on the classpath. It means that you need JDK to run Java, the app jars, and the dependencies, which also are named external JARs.

The JARs that make up the classpath are not necessarily interdependent on each other. In complex apps, complications were caused by packages that are scattered in more than jars, transitive dependencies, and accessibility problems. All of these problems are added to one category, namely The Jar Hell. This problem was resolved when Java9 was launched.

Access Modifiers

When you are declaring the type of an object in Java, you may configure who will be able to use the same. The Access modifiers tend to specify your access to the classes. In this case, we may say that you can use them at the top level. They also tend to specify your access to the members of the class. In this case, you use them at the member level. When you are using top-level, you can use only two modifiers, one is called public, and the other is called none.

At top-level class that you declare as public needs to be defined in the Java file with the same file name. That's why the following class named JavaX.java is stored under com.apress.bgn.ch0 package.

```
apress.bgn.ch0 package.
package com.apress.bgn.ch0;
//it is the top-level's access modifier
public class JavaX {
```

```
        . . .
    }
```

A public class can be seen by anyone anywhere. It always remains visible. The option to defy the use of an access modifier is called by the use of package-private and default modifier, which means that if the class lacks a modifier, it will only be visible to classes that are defined inside the same package. A class that lacks an access modifier may be defined in the Java file. The file must have the same name as that of the class. If you have declared a class JavaX in the X.java file, creating an object of the same type in the Main class is not possible.

You will still be able to write the code, but the Java compiler you are using will defy compiling it. There will be no bytecode for execution purposes. Java editors, who are smart, show you the error of ways by making the code painted red and also refusing to provide code resistance when you are writing it. A class that lacks an access modifier will be visible to all the classes inside the same package.

Inside a Java class, the members of the class are properly defined. These members are called methods and fields. The access modifiers are applied to the members of the class as well. At the member level, you apply two more modifiers known as protected and private, and the access modifiers carry the following effects on the code.

The first is public. It is the same spot as at the top level. You can access the members from everywhere in the code.

The second is known as private. The members may be accessed from inside their own class.

The third is known as protected. The member may only be accessed from inside the package or through a subclass of the class in some other package.

The fourth is none. Here you only can access the member from inside your own package.

It may appear to be highly complicated to you at the moment. However, the complications remain until you start writing the code.

Modules

In Java 9, developers were treated with the gift of modules. Modules are used for grouping and encapsulating the packages. The implementation of the new concept consumed a decade to develop. The discussion about the creation of modules began in 2005. They were proposed for Java7. A project, namely Project Jigsaw, was started as an exploratory phase in 2008. Java developers hoped that a modular JDK would enter the markets with Java8. However, they had to face disappointment. The release of the modules was only possible in Java9.

This is the reason the official release of Java9 was postponed until September 2017.

Modules in Java represent an innovative way to aggregate packages. A module is an innovative way to group all of them and also configure the granulated access to the contents of the package.

A module has a unique name. It is a reusable group of packages. There is a file name like the following: module-information.java. A module file carries the following information.

1. The first information is the name of the module.

2. The second is the dependencies of the module, like how many modules it depends on.

3. The third is packages it makes explicitly available to different other modules. All the other packages remain implicitly available to the other modules.

4. It shows the services it offers.

5. It carries the services it consumes.

6. It carries information of the native code.

7. It carries resources and configuration data.

In theory, naming the modules resemble the naming traditions of packages, and it follows the reversed-domain-name tradition. However, in practice, the module name has no number. Also, it clearly reveals its overall purpose. The module-info.java file compiles into module descriptor.

Configuring Modules

Modules depend on one another. The classes that are in the chapter.three module will be needing access to all the packages and to the classes in the chapter.zero modules. When you are declaring the dependency of a module, you need to use the *requires* keyword.

The preceding dependency is explicit. However, there are implicit dependencies as well. Any module that is declared by developers in an implicit way demands the JDK java.base module. Declaration of a module means that you need the module during the time of compilation and running time. If you need a module at the runtime, the static requires keywords are used for the declaration of the dependency. You need to keep in mind that it makes sense when you are dealing with web apps.

Just because a specific module depends on the other, it does not mean that it will have access to classes and packages. This is because the module it depends on needs to be configured for exposing the insides.

Chapter Two

Introduction to Java

You can use Java to develop desktop applications, mobile applications, gaming applications, and much more. Java is very popular among many computer languages. Oracle owns it, and there are over 3 billion devices that can be run on Java. Even database connections are created with Java.

Java can be run on any operating system like Linux, Raspberry Pi, Mac, and Windows, etc. The best thing about Java is that anybody can learn it and use it to build programs, as it is open-source and free to use. It is fast, secure, and powerful. It also has a sizable community support that consists of millions of developers. It is basically an object-oriented language that offers a clear structure to a number of programs. You also can reuse the code, which slashes your app development costs. Java is more like C# and C++, making it is easy for developers of C# and C++ to switch to Java easily.

Java Syntax

Here is the basic syntax of the simplest programs in Java.

19

```
public class JavaX {
  public static void main(String[] args) {
    System.out.println("I am about to start
learning Java.");
  }
}
```

```
I am about to start learning Java.
```

Each line in Java code must have a class. The line of code that misses a class is incomplete. In the above class, the class is named JavaX. The class name must start with an uppercase letter. Java is highly case-sensitive, which means that JavaX is different from javaX. The name of the Java file that you save on your computer system must have the name of the class as well. When you are saving a file, you should save it by using the name of the class and then add .java to the end of the name of the file. When you are about to run a code on your computer system, you need to ensure that Java is properly installed.

The main() Method

You can see that the example contains the main() method. It is required, and it is an integral part of each Java program. Any code that is inside the main() method must be executed. You need not study in detail the keywords that are placed before or after this method. I will explain them later on. At the simplest, keep in mind that the basic syntax of Java code has a class and a method. You can start from there and build the desired code.

Inside that method, you can use another method, namely printIn(), for printing a piece of text onto the screen. I have used one line of text. You can change the text and print it again. Let us try out a different piece of text and print it on the screen.

```
public class JavaX {
   public static void main(String[] args) {
      System.out.println("Like C++, Java is a
compiled language.");
   }
}

Like C++, Java is a compiled language.
```

Bear in mind that the curly braces denote the start and the end of a specific block of code. Each statement of code needs to end with a semicolon.

Java Comments

You can use Java comments to explain your code and to make it readable when you revisit your code. You can use the code to prevent the execution when you are testing a different code. When you use // before the start and end of a line, Java ignores it as a comment. Even if it is a code, Java will not execute it. The following example will use a single-line comment to explain the succeeding piece of code.

```
public class JavaX {
   public static void main(String[] args) {
      //The following line of code will
display a piece of text that appears inside
quotes.//
```

```
    System.out.println("Like C++, Java is a
compiled language.");
    }
}
```

```
Like C++, Java is a compiled language.
```

You also can use multiline comments in the code to explain a complicated piece of code. Multiline comments are different from single-line comments. A multiline comment starts with /* and concludes with */. Any piece of text that is in between /* and */ is outright ignored by Java.

```
public class JavaX {
    public static void main(String[] args) {
        /*The following line of code will
display a piece of text that appears inside
quotes.*/
        System.out.println("Like C++, Java is a
compiled language.");
    }
}
```

```
Like C++, Java is a compiled language.
```

There is no set rule for the use of single-line or multi-line comments. A general tradition for using comments is to use single-line for short comments and multi-line for longer comments.

Java Variables

Variables basically are containers to store data values. In Java, you will have many variables. Here is a rundown of Java variables.

1. A string variable is used to store different pieces of text. For example, 'Hello' is text. You can surround string values by using double-quotes.

2. The int variable stores different types of integers. These are whole numbers without decimals like -567 or -897.

3. A Boolean will store values that have two states. One will say true while the other will say false.

4. Int will store integers such as whole numbers. These are without decimals like -123 or 123.

5. The float will store the floating-point numbers like decimals such as -19.99 and 19.99.

Declaration of Variables

For the creation of Java variables, you need to specify what the type of the variable is and then assign the same with a particular value. In the syntax, the keyword variable denotes the name of the variable. It can be something like x or name. The equal sign is for assigning values to variables. You must take a look at the following example to create a variable that will store text. In the following example, I will create a variable and assign it a value.

```
public class JavaX {
  public static void main(String[] args) {
    String tez = "Java is a compiled
language which allows you to reuse the code
once it has been developed.";
    System.out.println(tez);
```

```
      }
   }
```

Java is a compiled language that allows you to reuse the code once it has been developed.

Let us see how you can create a variable and store in it a number to display.

```
public class JavaX {
  public static void main(String[] args) {
    int tezNum = 555;
    System.out.println(tezNum);
  }
}

555
```

You can see that I have changed the keyword from string to int to store and display a number.

Variable Without Assignment

You can create a variable, but you no longer have to assign it during the creation step. You can do that after it has been created. This works when you are building some complex pieces of code.

```
public class JavaX {
  public static void main(String[] args) {
    int tezNum;
    tezNum = 555;
    System.out.println(tezNum);
  }
}
555
```

There is a common problem with variables. If you assign an existing variable a new value, it tends to overwrite the existing value.

```
public class JavaX {
   public static void main(String[] args) {
      int tezNum = 555;
      tezNum = 777;
      System.out.println(tezNum);
   }
}
```

```
777
```

If you have already developed a code and you are concerned about someone overwriting the existing values, you can use the final keyword or the constant keyword to keep the values of variables from changing. The keywords final and constant mean read-only and unchangeable.

```
public class JavaX {
   public static void main(String[] args) {
      final int tezNum = 555;
      tezNum = 777;
      System.out.println(tezNum);
   }
}
```

JavaX.java:4: error: cannot assign a value to final variable tezNum

```
      tezNum = 777;
             ^
   1 error
```

The next piece of code contains the constant keyword.

```
public class JavaX {
  public static void main(String[] args) {
    constant int tezNum = 555;
    tezNum = 777;
    System.out.println(tezNum);
  }
}

JavaX.java:3: error: not a statement
    constant int tezNum = 555;
    ^
JavaX.java:3: error: ';' expected
    constant int tezNum = 555;
            ^
2 errors
```

Here is how you can declare float variable and assign value to the same.

```
public class JavaX {
  public static void main(String[] args) {
    float tezFloat = 555.555f;
    System.out.println(tezFloat);
  }
}

555.555
```

The following example shows how you can create a char variable and assign a value to the same.

```
public class JavaX {
  public static void main(String[] args) {
    char tezLetter = 'M';
```

```
      System.out.println(tezLetter);
   }
}
```

M

Here is an example of how you can create a Boolean variable and assign value to that.

```
public class JavaX {
   public static void main(String[] args) {
      boolean tezBool = true;
      System.out.println(tezBool);
   }
}
```

true

Chapter Three

Java Data Types

D ata types in Java are divided into a couple of groups. One group is named as primitive data types like short, bytes, float, long, boolean, double, char, and int. The second group is called non-primitive data types like String, Classes, and Arrays.

Primitive Data Types

The primitive data type generally specifies the type and size of the values of the variable. It does not contain any additional methods. See what the primitive data types are and how they are described.

- The first primitive data type is called byte. Its size is 1 byte and it stores all whole numbers starting from -128 and ending on 127.

```
public class JavaX {
public static void main(String[] args) {
  byte tezNum = 120;
  System.out.println(tezNum);
  }
}
120
```

- The second primitive data type is named as short. Its size is 2 bytes and it stores all whole numbers starting from -32,768 and ending on 32,767.

```
public class JavaX {
  public static void main(String[] args) {
    short tezNum = 30000;
    System.out.println(tezNum);
  }
}
```

```
30000
```

- The third primitive data type is called int. Its size is 4 byte and it stores all whole numbers starting from -2,147,483,648 and ending on 2,147,483,647.

```
public class JavaX {
  public static void main(String[] args) {
    int tezNum = 2200000;
    System.out.println(tezNum);
  }
}
```

```
2200000
```

- The fourth primitive data type is long. Its size is 8 bytes and it stores all whole numbers starting from -9,223,372,036,854,775,808 and ending on 9,223,372,036,854,775,807.

```
public class JavaX {
  public static void main(String[] args) {
    long tezNum = 300000000;
```

```
    System.out.println(tezNum);
  }
}
```

300000000

- The fifth primitive data type is called float. Its size is 4 bytes and it stores all fractional numbers that should be sufficient to store six to seven decimal digits.

```
public class JavaX {
  public static void main(String[] args) {
    float tezNum = 4.45f;
    System.out.println(tezNum);
  }
}
```

4.45

- The sixth primitive data type is called double. Its size is 8 bytes and it stores all fractional numbers starting from 15 decimal digits.

```
public class JavaX {
  public static void main(String[] args) {
    double tezNum = 24.45d;
    System.out.println(tezNum);
  }
}
```

24.45

- The seventh primitive data type is called boolean. Its size is 1 bit, and it stores only true and false values.

- The eighth primitive data type is called char. Its size is 2 bytes, and it stores a single character or letter or ASCII values.

The String datatype in Java is so much integrated into the language that programmers dub it as the ninth type. A string is a non-primitive data type because it alludes to an object. The String object carries multiple methods that are handy in performing different types of operations in strings.

Non-Primitive Data Types

Non-primitive data types are also known as reference types because they tend to refer to objects. The major difference between the two data types is that primitive types have been pre-defined in Java. However, the non-primitive data types are created by programmers. Except for String, Java does not pre-define any of them.

Non-primitive data types are used to call different methods to perform a number of operations, while primitive data types cannot do that. A primitive data type has a value, while a non-primitive data type may be null at times. You always have to start a primitive data type with a lowercase letter, while you always have to start a non-primitive data type with an uppercase letter. This also works well for differentiating different data types.

Java Type Casting

Type casting happens when you assign a certain value of a primitive data type to another one. There are two casting types in

Java. The first type is known as Widening Casting, used to convert a smaller type into a bigger type size.

The second type is the narrowing casting type that happens manually. It is used to convert a bigger type into a smaller type.

You can do widening casting when you pass a smaller size data type to a bigger size data type.

```
public class JavaX {
  public static void main(String[] args) {
    int tezInt = 19;
    double tezDouble = tezInt; // This is an
example of Automatic casting: I am
converting int into double

    System.out.println(tezInt);
    System.out.println(tezDouble);
  }
}

19
19.0
```

Now let us check out how narrowing casting works. It needs to be done manually by putting a data type in parentheses before the value.

```
public class JavaX {
  public static void main(String[] args) {
    double tezDouble = 19; // This is an
example of manual casting: I am converting
double into int
    int tezInt = (int) tezDouble;
```

```
    System.out.println(tezDouble);
    System.out.println(tezInt);
  }
}

19.0
19
```

Chapter Four

Java Operators & Java Strings

Operators are used to perform different operations on certain values and variables. For example, you can use the + operator to combine two values.

```java
public class JavaX {
  public static void main(String[] args) {
    int a = 150 + 500;
    System.out.println(a);
  }
}
```

```
650
```

The + operator is used for adding two values as it did in the above example, it may be used to add a variable and a value. It may also be used to pair up a variable with another variable.

```java
public class JavaX {
  public static void main(String[] args) {
    int summing1 = 1000 + 10;
    int summing2 = summing1 + 550;
    int summing3 = summing2 + summing2;
    System.out.println(summing1);
```

```
        System.out.println(summing2);
        System.out.println(summing3);
    }
}

1010
1560
3120
```

Arithmetic Operators

One is addition. You have seen how it works in the above example. The second arithmetic operator is subtraction. It is used to extract one value from another. I will use the same example to show how this one works.

```
public class JavaX {
    public static void main(String[] args) {
        int summing1 = 1000 - 10;
        int summing2 = summing1 - 550;
        int summing3 = summing2 - 11;
        System.out.println(summing1);
        System.out.println(summing2);
        System.out.println(summing3);
    }
}

990
440
429
```

The third arithmetic operator is for multiplication of two values. See how it works.

```
public class JavaX {
```

```
public static void main(String[] args) {
    int xx = 50;
    int yy = 30;
    System.out.println(xx * yy);
}
}
```

```
1500
```

The fourth arithmetic operator is about division of two values. One value is divided by another one to get the result.

```
public class JavaX {
    public static void main(String[] args) {
        int xx = 48;
        int yy = 12;
        System.out.println(xx / yy);
    }
}
```

```
4
```

The following arithmetic operator is used to calculate the modulus of the numbers.

```
public class JavaX {
    public static void main(String[] args) {
        int xx = 50;
        int yy = 12;
        System.out.println(xx % yy);
    }
}
```

```
2
```

This arithmetic operator will increment of the value by one number.

```
public class JavaX {
  public static void main(String[] args) {
    int xx = 50;
    ++xx;
    System.out.println(xx);
  }
}
```

51

The arithmetic operator -- is used to cut down the value of the variable by a single number. See the following example.

```
public class JavaX {
  public static void main(String[] args) {
    int xx = 50;
    --xx;
    System.out.println(xx);
  }
}
```

49

All the code is the same except the operator. It has decreased the number one. The operators are very useful and almost necessary to use in Java. They are integral to performing important mathematical calculations.

Java Strings

You can use Java strings to store pieces of text. A string may carry a collection of different characters that are surrounded by double-quotes. In the next example, I will create a string variable and then assign it a value.

```
public class JavaX {
  public static void main(String[] args) {
    String msg = "Strings are the most
commonly used data type in Java and other
programming languages.";
    System.out.println(msg);
  }
}
```

Strings are the most commonly used data type in Java and other programming languages.

In the world of Java, a string is generally used in the form of an object. It contains certain methods that tend to perform many operations regarding strings. You can find the total length of a string by using the length() method.

```
public class JavaX {
  public static void main(String[] args) {
    String msg = "Strings are the most
commonly used data type in Java and other
programming languages.";
    System.out.println(msg);
    System.out.println("the length of the
above mentioned string is : " +
msg.length());
  }
}
```

Strings are the most commonly used data type in Java and other programming languages.

```
the length of the above-mentioned string is:
84
```

38

String Methods

The string is amazing in the sense that you can find a wide range of methods to experiment with the pieces of text you add to your code. In the next example, I will experiment with the upper case and lower case methods to change the case of the code.

```
public class JavaX {
   public static void main(String[] args) {
     String msg = "Strings are the most
commonly used data type in Java and other
programming languages.";
     System.out.println(msg.toUpperCase());
     System.out.println(msg.toLowerCase());
   }
}
```

STRINGS ARE THE MOST COMMONLY USED DATA TYPE IN JAVA AND OTHER PROGRAMMING LANGUAGES.

Strings are the most commonly used data type in java and other programming languages.

You can find a certain character inside of a string. The indexOf() string method will return the index number of the very first occurrence of a specific text inside a string. The method applies to whitespaces.

```
public class JavaX {
   public static void main(String[] args) {
     String msg = "Strings are the most
commonly used data type in Java and other
programming languages.";
     System.out.println(msg.indexOf("Java"));
```

```
        }
    }
```

48

The index number starts at zero, which is why Java counts the index position from zero and goes onward.

Concatenation Process

You can use the addition operator to add one string to another. This may sound odd, but it is possible. The + operator adds not only two numbers but also two strings as well. The process of adding one string into another is called string concatenation. The method is useful, especially when you have to take the input from users and combine it so that it makes sense when you store it in the database. It refines raw input and makes it readable. The following example will help explain how you can use the concatenation method to combine strings.

```
public class JavaX {
    public static void main(String args[]) {
        String fName = "Astral";
        String lName = "Tree";
        System.out.println("My full name is " +
fName + " " + lName + ". You can call me
Astro in short.");
    }
}
```

My full name is Astral Tree. You can call me Astro in short.

If you don't want to use the + operator to concatenate two strings, you can use the concat() method to do so. It will perform the same function.

```
public class JavaX {
  public static void main(String args[]) {
    String fName = "Astral ";
    String lName = "Tree";
    System.out.println("My full name is " +
fName.concat(lName) + ". You can call me
Astro in short.");
  }
}
```

My full name is Astral Tree. You can call me Astro in short.

Special Character Confusion

You should keep in mind that strings are always enclosed inside double-quotes. While this makes the identification of strings easier, this also creates a great deal of confusion when you have to use some special characters inside strings. Java will not recognize any special character and generate an error in return. So, there is a way out. You can use backslash escape characters, which turn special characters into string characters. The escape character \' will create a single quote. The escape character \" will create a double quote, and the \\ will create a backslash.

```
public class JavaX {
  public static void main(String[] args) {
    String msg = "String is the most useful
data type in \"Java\".";
    System.out.println(msg);
  }
```

```
    }

    String is the most useful data type in
    "Java."
```

Let us see how we can add a single quote to the string and what result it brings for us.

```
public class JavaX {
   public static void main(String[] args) {
     String msg = "It is String\'s job to
allow programmers to integrate text into the
code.";
     System.out.println(msg);
   }
}
```

It is String's job to allow programmers to integrate text into the code.

Let us try out some more escape characters that can help us write better code when we are developing a program.

```
public class JavaX {
   public static void main(String[] args) {
     String msg = "String is the most useful
data type in \"Java\." \nIt offers many
methods to do experiments with.";
     System.out.println(msg);
   }
}

String is the most useful data type in
"Java."
```

It offers many methods to do experiments
with.

The second escape character is for carriage return.

```
public class JavaX {
  public static void main(String[] args) {
    String msg = "String is the most useful
data type in \"Java\." \rIt offers many
methods to do experiments with.";
    System.out.println(msg);
  }
}
```

```
String is the most useful data type in
"Java."
It offers many methods to do experiments
with.
```

Here is how you can add a tab in between the text. The escape
character you have to use is \t. See the following example to have a
better understanding of the code.

```
public class JavaX {
  public static void main(String[] args) {
    String msg = "String is the \tmost
useful data type in \"Java\." \tIt offers
many methods \to do experiments with.";
    System.out.println(msg);
  }
}
```

```
String is the most useful data type in
"Java."    It offers many methods to do
experiments with.
```

There is an escape character \b that performs the function of the backspace key on the computer keyboard. It will delete one character to the back of its position. You have to place it right after the letter you want to do away with.

Java Mathematics

Java math has several methods that help you perform many mathematical tasks when you are dealing with numbers. The first method to do mathematical functions helps you find the highest value of two numbers.

```
public class JavaX {
  public static void main(String[] args) {
    System.out.println(Math.max(1444, 55));
  }
}
```

```
1444
```

You can use the mini method to find out the lowest number of the two. See how it works. I will use the same code example. The only difference is that I will replace max with min keyword.

```
public class JavaX {
  public static void main(String[] args) {
    System.out.println(Math.min(1444, 55));
  }
}
```

```
55
```

Java Arrays

Java offers a specific data structure, the array, to programmers. Arrays store fixed-size collections of the same types. They are written and stored in a proper sequence. An array is defined as a data collection. However, it is more appropriate to consider it a collection of variables of the same type. Instead of declaring individual variables like number0, number1, and number50, you need to declare one variable in the array like a number[0] for the representation of individual variables.

Declaration of Array Variables

When you want to use a specific array in a particular program, you need to declare a variable for referencing an array. You also need to specify the array type that the variable can refer to.

When you are processing the elements of an array, you often need to use the for loop or the foreach loop because all the elements of the array share the same type. The size of the array is also clearly known.

```java
public class TestingTheArray {

    public static void main(String[] args) {
        double[] TezList = {2.9, 5.9, 6.4,
    6.5};

        // In this step I will Print the array
    elements
        for (int x = 0; x < TezList.length;
    x++) {
```

```
        System.out.println(TezList[x] + "
");
        }

        // Here I will sum up all the elements
        double Thetotal = 0;
        for (int x = 0; x < TezList.length;
x++) {
                Thetotal += TezList[x];
        }
        System.out.println("Here is the total
of the array: " + Thetotal);

        // Finding the largest element
        double maximum = TezList[0];
        for (int x = 1; x < TezList.length;
x++) {
                if (TezList[x] > maximum) maximum =
TezList[x];
        }
        System.out.println("The Maximum value
of the array is " + maximum);
        }
}

2.9
5.9
6.4
6.5
Here is the total of the array:
21.700000000000003
The Maximum value of the array is 6.5
```

Here is the function of the for loop in Java arrays. The for loop will print all the elements of the array.

```
public class TestingTheArray {

    public static void main(String[] args) {
        double[] TezList = {2.9, 5.9, 6.4,
6.5};

        // This code will Print the array
elements
        for (double element: TezList) {
            System.out.println(element);
        }
    }
}

2.9
5.9
6.4
6.5
```

Java ArrayList

The ArrayList in Java is a class that is used for the resizable array. You can use the java.util package to find the ArrayList class. There is a difference between the Java built-in array and the ArrayList class. The size of the array cannot be modified at all. If you have built a program that demands that you add or remove certain elements in an array, you need to have a custom array. ArrayList allows you to add or remove as many elements from an array as you need to.

Adding Items

The ArrayList class carries a number of useful methods. If you need to add elements to the ArrayList class, you can use add() method.

```java
import java.util.ArrayList;

public class Main {
  public static void main(String[] args) {
    ArrayList<String> vegetables = new
ArrayList<String>();
    vegetables.add( " pumpkin " );
    vegetables.add( " tomato " );
    vegetables.add( " ginger " );
    vegetables.add( " potato " );
    vegetables.add( " okra " );
    vegetables.add( " garlic " );
    vegetables.add( " onion " );
    vegetables.add( " cabbage " );
    System.out.println(vegetables);
  }
}
```

```
[ pumpkin, tomato, ginger, potato, okra,
garlic, onion, cabbage ]
```

You can access the item of your choice from an ArrayList. See the following method. The name of the method is the get() method. See how to use it in the code.

```java
import java.util.ArrayList;

public class Main {
  public static void main(String[] args) {
    ArrayList<String> vegetables = new
ArrayList<String>();
    vegetables.add( " pumpkin " );
    vegetables.add( " tomato " );
    vegetables.add( " ginger " );
    vegetables.add( " potato " );
    vegetables.add( " okra " );
```

```
      vegetables.add( " garlic " );
      vegetables.add( " onion " );
      vegetables.add( " cabbage " );
      System.out.println(vegetables);
      System.out.println(vegetables.get(0));
      System.out.println(vegetables.get(1));
      System.out.println(vegetables.get(3));
      System.out.println(vegetables.get(5));
      System.out.println(vegetables.get(6));
   }
}


[ pumpkin, tomato, ginger, potato, okra,
garlic, onion, cabbage ]
 pumpkin
 tomato
 potato
 garlic
 onion
```

The index starts with zero and not one. You can modify any element in the array by replacing it with a new one. However, you have to remember the index number of the array element to modify it perfectly. If you enter the wrong index number, you are unlikely to get a perfect replacement. See the technique to do that. The method I will use is known as the set() method. You will see two lists in the output; one is the original array list, and the other is the modified list.

```
import java.util.ArrayList;

public class Main {
   public static void main(String[] args) {
```

```java
    ArrayList<String> vegetables = new
ArrayList<String>();
    vegetables.add( " pumpkin " );
    vegetables.add( " tomato " );
    vegetables.add( " ginger " );
    vegetables.add( " potato " );
    vegetables.add( " okra " );
    vegetables.add( " garlic " );
    vegetables.add( " onion " );
    vegetables.add( " cabbage " );
    System.out.println(vegetables);
    vegetables.set(0, " cilantro ");
    vegetables.set(1, " radish ");
    vegetables.set(2, " carrot ");
    vegetables.set(3, " eggplant ");
    vegetables.set(4, " capsicum ");
    System.out.println(vegetables);

    }
}


[ pumpkin, tomato, ginger, potato, okra,
garlic, onion, cabbage ]
[ cilantro, radish, carrot, eggplant,
capsicum, garlic, onion, cabbage ]
```

Just as you can add different elements to an existing array list, you can also remove items from the list. For removing elements from the array list, you will have to use the remove() method. Here once again, we need the index number to get started.

```java
import java.util.ArrayList;

public class Main {
    public static void main(String[] args) {
```

```java
        ArrayList<String> vegetables = new
ArrayList<String>();
    vegetables.add( " pumpkin " );
    vegetables.add( " tomato " );
    vegetables.add( " ginger " );
    vegetables.add( " potato " );
    vegetables.add( " okra " );
    vegetables.add( " garlic " );
    vegetables.add( " onion " );
    vegetables.add( " cabbage " );
    vegetables.add( " cilantro ");
    vegetables.add( " radish ");
    vegetables.add( " carrot ");
    vegetables.add( " eggplant ");
    System.out.println(vegetables);
    vegetables.remove(0);
    System.out.println(vegetables);
    vegetables.remove(2);
    System.out.println(vegetables);
    vegetables.remove(4);
    System.out.println(vegetables);
    vegetables.remove(6);
    System.out.println(vegetables);
    vegetables.remove(7);
    System.out.println(vegetables);
  }
}
```

[pumpkin, tomato, ginger, potato, okra,
garlic, onion, cabbage, cilantro, radish,
carrot, eggplant]
[tomato, ginger, potato, okra, garlic,
onion, cabbage, cilantro, radish, carrot,
eggplant]

```
[ tomato, ginger, okra, garlic, onion,
cabbage, cilantro, radish, carrot, eggplant
]
[ tomato, ginger, okra, garlic, cabbage,
cilantro, radish, carrot, eggplant ]
[ tomato, ginger, okra, garlic, cabbage,
cilantro, carrot, eggplant ]
[ tomato, ginger, okra, garlic, cabbage,
cilantro, carrot ]
```

If you want empty an array of all the elements, you can use the clear() method. See how to do that.

```
import java.util.ArrayList;

public class Main {
  public static void main(String[] args) {
    ArrayList<String> vegetables = new
ArrayList<String>();
    vegetables.add( " pumpkin " );
    vegetables.add( " tomato " );
    vegetables.add( " ginger " );
    vegetables.add( " potato " );
    vegetables.add( " okra " );
    vegetables.add( " garlic " );
    vegetables.add( " onion " );
    vegetables.add( " cabbage " );
    vegetables.add( " cilantro ");
    vegetables.add( " radish ");
    vegetables.add( " carrot ");
    vegetables.add( " eggplant ");
    System.out.println(vegetables);
    vegetables.clear();
    System.out.println(vegetables);
```

```
        }
    }
```

```
[ pumpkin, tomato, ginger, potato, okra,
garlic, onion, cabbage, cilantro, radish,
carrot, eggplant ]
[]
```

You can find out the total size of an array list by using the size method.

```
import java.util.ArrayList;

public class Main {
    public static void main(String[] args) {
        ArrayList<String> vegetables = new
ArrayList<String>();
        vegetables.add( " pumpkin " );
        vegetables.add( " tomato " );
        vegetables.add( " ginger " );
        vegetables.add( " potato " );
        vegetables.add( " okra " );
        vegetables.add( " garlic " );
        vegetables.add( " onion " );
        vegetables.add( " cabbage " );
        vegetables.add( " cilantro ");
        vegetables.add( " radish ");
        vegetables.add( " carrot ");
        vegetables.add( " eggplant ");
        System.out.println(vegetables.size());
    }
}
```

```
12
```

Looping ArrayLists

You can create a loop through the arraylist. The for loop will iterate through all the elements and display them neatly on the screen. You also can add to the code the size() method to specify the number of times you have looped through the arraylist.

```java
import java.util.ArrayList;

public class Main {
  public static void main(String[] args) {
    ArrayList<String> vegetables = new
ArrayList<String>();
    vegetables.add( " pumpkin " );
    vegetables.add( " tomato " );
    vegetables.add( " ginger " );
    vegetables.add( " potato " );
    vegetables.add( " okra " );
    vegetables.add( " garlic " );
    vegetables.add( " onion " );
    vegetables.add( " cabbage " );
    vegetables.add( " cilantro ");
    vegetables.add( " radish ");
    vegetables.add( " carrot ");
    vegetables.add( " eggplant ");
    for (int x = 0; x < vegetables.size();
x++) {
      System.out.println(vegetables.get(x));
    }
    }
}

pumpkin
 tomato
 ginger
 potato
```

```
okra
garlic
onion
cabbage
cilantro
radish
carrot
egg plant
```

You also can use the for-each loop to iterate through the ArrayList. The result with the same but the method to reach that result is different.

```java
import java.util.ArrayList;

public class Main {
  public static void main(String[] args) {
    ArrayList<String> vegetables = new
ArrayList<String>();
    vegetables.add( " pumpkin " );
    vegetables.add( " tomato " );
    vegetables.add( " ginger " );
    vegetables.add( " potato " );
    vegetables.add( " okra " );
    vegetables.add( " garlic " );
    vegetables.add( " onion " );
    vegetables.add( " cabbage " );
    vegetables.add( " cilantro ");
    vegetables.add( " radish ");
    vegetables.add( " carrot ");
    vegetables.add( " eggplant ");
    for (String x : vegetables) {
      System.out.println(x);
    }
  }
}
```

```
pumpkin
 tomato
 ginger
 potato
 okra
 garlic
 onion
 cabbage
 cilantro
 radish
 carrot
 egg plant
```

I have used strings as objects in the above examples. You can use other types as well. A string is an object but never a primitive type. To use different other types like int, you need to specify the class Integer. You also can use Boolean, Character, and Double etc. You can create the ArrayList for storing numbers like adding elements of different types like Integers.

```
import java.util.ArrayList;

public class Main {
  public static void main(String[] args) {
    ArrayList<Integer> TezNumbers = new
ArrayList<Integer>();
    TezNumbers.add(7);
    TezNumbers.add(14);
    TezNumbers.add(21);
    TezNumbers.add(28);
    TezNumbers.add(35);
    TezNumbers.add(42);
    for (int x : TezNumbers) {
      System.out.println(x);
```

```
      }
   }
}

7
14
21
28
35
42
```

Sorting

There is another useful class in java.until package. It is known as Collections class. It includes sort() method to sort out lists alphabetically or numerically.

```java
import java.util.ArrayList;
import java.util.Collections;

public class Main {
  public static void main(String[] args) {
    ArrayList<String> vegetables = new
ArrayList<String>();
    vegetables.add( " pumpkin " );
    vegetables.add( " tomato " );
    vegetables.add( " ginger " );
    vegetables.add( " potato " );
    vegetables.add( " okra " );
    vegetables.add( " garlic " );
    vegetables.add( " onion " );
    vegetables.add( " cabbage " );
    vegetables.add( " cilantro ");
    vegetables.add( " radish ");
    vegetables.add( " carrot ");
    vegetables.add( " eggplant ");
```

```
      Collections.sort(vegetables);

      for (String x : vegetables) {
        System.out.println(x);
      }
    }
}
```

```
cabbage
 carrot
 cilantro
 egg plant
 garlic
 ginger
 okra
 onion
 potato
 pumpkin
 radish
 tomato
```

Similarly, you can sort out an arraylist of numbers.

```
import java.util.ArrayList;
import java.util.Collections;

public class Main {
  public static void main(String[] args) {
    ArrayList<Integer> TezNumbers = new
ArrayList<Integer>();
    TezNumbers.add(39);
    TezNumbers.add(19);
    TezNumbers.add(23);
    TezNumbers.add(84);
    TezNumbers.add(48);
    TezNumbers.add(32);
```

```
    Collections.sort(TezNumbers);

    for (int x : TezNumbers) {
      System.out.println(x);
    }
  }
}

19
23
32
39
48
84
```

LinkedList

Here is an example of the linked list that is almost identical to arraylist.

```
import java.util.LinkedList;

public class Main {
  public static void main(String[] args) {
    LinkedList<String> vegetables = new
LinkedList<String>();
    vegetables.add( " pumpkin " );
    vegetables.add( " tomato " );
    vegetables.add( " ginger " );
    vegetables.add( " potato " );
    vegetables.add( " okra " );
    vegetables.add( " garlic " );
    vegetables.add( " onion " );
    vegetables.add( " cabbage " );
    vegetables.add( " cilantro ");
```

```
        vegetables.add( " radish ");
        vegetables.add( " carrot ");
        vegetables.add( " eggplant ");
          System.out.println(vegetables);


    }

}
```

```
[ pumpkin, tomato, ginger, potato, okra,
garlic, onion, cabbage, cilantro, radish,
carrot, eggplant ]
```

A LinkedList is a collection that contains different objects of same type. This feature brings it closer to the ArrayList. The LinkedList class welcomes all the methods that an ArrayList uses because both of them implement List interface. This means that you have the opportunity to add items, remove items, change items, and similarly clear the entire list. Their applications are the same. It is only their built, which is different. I will apply a couple of methods in the following examples to show how the usage of both is the same.

Here is an example of the remove method for LinkedLists.

```
    import java.util.LinkedList;

public class Main {
   public static void main(String[] args) {
      LinkedList<String> vegetables = new
LinkedList<String>();
      vegetables.add( " pumpkin " );
      vegetables.add( " tomato " );
      vegetables.add( " ginger " );
      vegetables.add( " potato " );
      vegetables.add( " okra " );
```

```
            vegetables.add( " garlic " );
            vegetables.add( " onion " );
            vegetables.add( " cabbage " );
            vegetables.add( " cilantro ");
            vegetables.add( " radish ");
            vegetables.add( " carrot ");
            vegetables.add( " eggplant ");
            vegetables.remove(0);
            System.out.println(vegetables);
            vegetables.remove(1);
            System.out.println(vegetables);
            vegetables.remove(2);
            System.out.println(vegetables);
            vegetables.remove(3);
            System.out.println(vegetables);

        }
    }
```

```
[ tomato, ginger, potato, okra, garlic,
onion, cabbage, cilantro, radish, carrot,
eggplant ]
[ tomato, potato, okra, garlic, onion,
cabbage, cilantro, radish, carrot, eggplant
]
[ tomato, potato, garlic, onion, cabbage,
cilantro, radish, carrot, eggplant ]
[ tomato, potato, garlic, cabbage, cilantro,
radish, carrot, eggplant ]
```

A LinkedList is the collection that may contain several similar objects just like ArrayList. A LinkedList class carries the same methods such as the ArrayList because both implement a List interface. Just like lists do, you can add, remove and modify elements in both of them. Use ArrayList when you need to access different items randomly and frequently or remove or add elements at the end of a list. Use LinkedList when you have to loop through instead of accessing items randomly.

Some methods make LinkedList different from ArrayList. You can use the addfirst method to insert certain elements to the start of the LinkedList, which is not included in the ArrayLists.

```java
import java.util.LinkedList;

public class Main {
  public static void main(String[] args) {
    LinkedList<String> vegetables = new
LinkedList<String>();
    vegetables.add( " pumpkin " );
    vegetables.add( " tomato " );
    vegetables.add( " ginger " );
    vegetables.add( " potato " );
    vegetables.add( " okra " );
    vegetables.add( " garlic " );
    vegetables.add( " eggplant ");
    vegetables.addFirst("cilantro");
    System.out.println(vegetables);
    vegetables.addFirst("radish");
    System.out.println(vegetables);
    vegetables.addFirst("carrot");
    System.out.println(vegetables);
  }
}

[cilantro, pumpkin, tomato, ginger, potato,
okra, garlic, eggplant ]
[radish, cilantro, pumpkin, tomato, ginger,
potato, okra, garlic, eggplant ]
```

```
[carrot, radish, cilantro, pumpkin, tomato,
ginger, potato, okra, garlic, eggplant ]
```

Similarly, the addlast() method helps you add items to the end of the list.

```
import java.util.LinkedList;

public class Main {
  public static void main(String[] args) {
    LinkedList<String> vegetables = new
LinkedList<String>();
    vegetables.add( " pumpkin " );
    vegetables.add( " tomato " );
    vegetables.add( " garlic " );
    vegetables.add( " eggplant ");
    vegetables.addLast("cilantro");
    System.out.println(vegetables);
    vegetables.addLast("radish");
    System.out.println(vegetables);
    vegetables.addLast("carrot");
    System.out.println(vegetables);
  }
}
```

```
[ pumpkin, tomato, garlic, eggplant,
cilantro]
[ pumpkin, tomato, garlic, eggplant,
cilantro, radish]
[ pumpkin, tomato, garlic, eggplant,
cilantro, radish, carrot]
```

While we are bound to remove elements in ArrayList through index number the LinkedList allows us to remove methods from the start of the end of the list. This is interesting and highly useful if you don't have index numbers to remove items. You can just use these two methods and slice off the items you don't need in the list. I will use both methods to remove items in the following example.

```java
import java.util.LinkedList;

public class Main {
  public static void main(String[] args) {
    LinkedList<String> vegetables = new
LinkedList<String>();
    vegetables.add( " pumpkin " );
    vegetables.add( " tomato " );
    vegetables.add( " ginger " );
    vegetables.add( " potato " );
    vegetables.add( " okra " );
    vegetables.add( " garlic " );
    vegetables.add( " eggplant ");
    vegetables.removeFirst();
    System.out.println(vegetables);
    vegetables.removeFirst();
    System.out.println(vegetables);
    vegetables.removeLast();
    System.out.println(vegetables);
    vegetables.removeLast();
    System.out.println(vegetables);
  }
}

[ tomato, ginger, potato, okra, garlic,
eggplant ]
[ ginger, potato, okra, garlic, eggplant ]
[ ginger, potato, okra, garlic ]
[ ginger, potato, okra ]
```

Similarly, you don't need an index number to display items from the list. You can use the get method to display items from the start and end of the list.

```java
import java.util.LinkedList;

public class Main {
  public static void main(String[] args) {
    LinkedList<String> vegetables = new
LinkedList<String>();
    vegetables.add( " pumpkin " );
    vegetables.add( " tomato " );
    vegetables.add( " ginger " );
    vegetables.add( " potato " );
    vegetables.add( " okra " );
    vegetables.add( " garlic " );
    vegetables.add( " eggplant ");

System.out.println(vegetables.getFirst());

System.out.println(vegetables.removeFirst())
;

System.out.println(vegetables.getFirst());

System.out.println(vegetables.getLast());

System.out.println(vegetables.removeLast());

System.out.println(vegetables.getLast());
  }
}

pumpkin
 pumpkin
 tomato
```

```
egg plant
egg plant
garlic
```

Hash Map

A hash map allows you to add items to the code in the form of key-value pairs. You can later on access them. You can use one object as key to another value known as value. It will store different types like strings, integers and other similar types.

```java
import java.util.HashMap;

public class Main {
    public static void main(String[] args) {
        HashMap<String, String> famousCities =
new HashMap<String, String>();
        famousCities.put("England",
"Manchester");
        famousCities.put("Germany", "Berlin");
        famousCities.put("Italy", "Rome");
        famousCities.put("USA", "New York");
        famousCities.put("South Africa", "Cape
Town");
        famousCities.put("India", "Mumbai");
        famousCities.put("Pakistan", "Lahore");
        System.out.println(famousCities);
    }
}

{USA=New York, Pakistan=Lahore,
England=Manchester, Italy=Rome, South
Africa=Cape Town, Germany=Berlin,
India=Mumbai}
```

If you have to access a specific item from the Hash map, you have to use the get() method and display the item.

```java
import java.util.HashMap;

public class Main {
  public static void main(String[] args) {
    HashMap<String, String> famousCities =
new HashMap<String, String>();
    famousCities.put("England",
"Manchester");
    famousCities.put("Germany", "Berlin");
    famousCities.put("Italy", "Rome");
    famousCities.put("USA", "New York");
    famousCities.put("India", "Mumbai");
    famousCities.put("Pakistan", "Lahore");

System.out.println(famousCities.get("USA"));

System.out.println(famousCities.get("Italy")
);
  }
}

New York
Rome
```

I will use the remove() method to remove items from the hash map.

```java
import java.util.HashMap;

public class Main {
  public static void main(String[] args) {
    HashMap<String, String> famousCities =
new HashMap<String, String>();
```

```
        famousCities.put("England",
"Manchester");
        famousCities.put("Germany", "Berlin");
        famousCities.put("Italy", "Rome");
        famousCities.put("USA", "New York");
        famousCities.put("India", "Mumbai");
        famousCities.put("Pakistan", "Lahore");
        famousCities.remove("England");
        System.out.println(famousCities);
        famousCities.remove("India");
        System.out.println(famousCities);
        famousCities.remove("Germany");
        System.out.println(famousCities);
    }
}

{USA=New York, Pakistan=Lahore, Italy=Rome,
Germany=Berlin, India=Mumbai}
{USA=New York, Pakistan=Lahore, Italy=Rome,
Germany=Berlin}
{USA=New York, Pakistan=Lahore, Italy=Rome}
```

If you want to remove all items from Hash map, you have to use the clear() method.

```
import java.util.HashMap;

public class Main {
  public static void main(String[] args) {
    HashMap<String, String> famousCities =
new HashMap<String, String>();
    famousCities.put("England",
"Manchester");
    famousCities.put("Germany", "Berlin");
    famousCities.put("Italy", "Rome");
    famousCities.put("USA", "New York");
```

```
        famousCities.put("India", "Mumbai");
        famousCities.put("Pakistan", "Lahore");
        famousCities.remove("England");
        System.out.println(famousCities);
        famousCities.clear();
        System.out.println(famousCities);
    }
}
```

```
{USA=New York, Pakistan=Lahore, Italy=Rome,
Germany=Berlin, India=Mumbai}
{}
```

The size() method is used to find out the total size of the hash map.

```
import java.util.HashMap;

public class Main {
  public static void main(String[] args) {
    HashMap<String, String> famousCities =
new HashMap<String, String>();
    famousCities.put("England",
"Manchester");
    famousCities.put("Germany", "Berlin");
    famousCities.put("Italy", "Rome");
    famousCities.put("USA", "New York");
    famousCities.put("India", "Mumbai");
    famousCities.put("Pakistan", "Lahore");
    System.out.println(famousCities.size());
  }
}
```

```
6
```

You also can create a loop through all the items of HashMap. I will build a for-each loop in the following example and let it run its course through the items of the hashmap. The method used for the purpose is called keyset() method. However, it is only perfect if you need the keys only. You can use values() method if you need to use the values as well.

```java
import java.util.HashMap;

public class Main {
  public static void main(String[] args) {
    HashMap<String, String> famousCities =
new HashMap<String, String>();
    famousCities.put("England",
"Manchester");
    famousCities.put("Germany", "Berlin");
    famousCities.put("Italy", "Rome");
    famousCities.put("USA", "New York");
    famousCities.put("India", "Mumbai");
    famousCities.put("Pakistan", "Lahore");

    for (String x : famousCities.keySet()) {
      System.out.println(x);
    }
  }
}
```

```
USA
Pakistan
England
Italy
Germany
India
```

We also can print the values through the for-each loop. See the following example.

```
import java.util.HashMap;

public class Main {
  public static void main(String[] args) {
    HashMap<String, String> famousCities =
new HashMap<String, String>();
    famousCities.put("England",
"Manchester");
    famousCities.put("Germany", "Berlin");
    famousCities.put("Italy", "Rome");
    famousCities.put("USA", "New York");
    famousCities.put("India", "Mumbai");
    famousCities.put("Pakistan", "Lahore");

    for (String x : famousCities.values()) {
      System.out.println(x);
    }
  }
}

New York
Lahore
Manchester
Rome
Berlin
Mumbai
```

You can use both keys and values to produce in an output. The following example will explain its usage.

```
import java.util.HashMap;

public class Main {
  public static void main(String[] args) {
    HashMap<String, String> famousCities =
new HashMap<String, String>();
```

```
    famousCities.put("England",
"Manchester");
    famousCities.put("Germany", "Berlin");
    famousCities.put("Italy", "Rome");
    famousCities.put("USA", "New York");
    famousCities.put("India", "Mumbai");
    famousCities.put("Pakistan", "Lahore");

    for (String x : famousCities.keySet()) {
      System.out.println("Last year I
travelled to " + x + ". I found  " +
famousCities.get(x) + " city to be the most
beautiful and hospitable.");
    }
  }
}
```

Last year I travelled to USA. I found New York city to be the most beautiful and hospitable.

Last year I travelled to Pakistan. I found Lahore city to be the most beautiful and hospitable.

Last year I travelled to England. I found Manchester city to be the most beautiful and hospitable.

Last year I travelled to Italy. I found Rome city to be the most beautiful and hospitable.

Last year I travelled to Germany. I found Berlin city to be the most beautiful and hospitable.

Last year I travelled to India. I found Mumbai city to be the most beautiful and hospitable.

Chapter Five

Java Conditionals
& Switch Statement

You have learned how to create statements and which types of operators you must use. Elements of logic must be added at times to run the code and keep it running without interruption. This chapter will walk you through the process of manipulating the code execution, using conditional statements and repetitive statements to achieve the goal. You can represent an algorithm and a solution by using flowcharts.

Java supports the logical conditions in mathematics. Here is a rundown of the conditions that you can use in the codes in Java. You can use the less than condition x<y, the less than and equal to sign x <= y, the greater than sign x > y, the greater than or equal condition x >= y, the equal to condition x == y, and the not equal to condition x != y.

You can use all these conditions for performing a set of actions for various reasons. For example, the if statement helps you specify a certain block of code that must be executed in case a specified condition turns out to be true. You can use the else statement to specify the code that must execute if a condition returns false. You can use the else if statement for specifying and testing a condition in case of false condition. You can use the switch statement for specifying different codes that must be executed.

The if Statement

You can use the if statement if you want a specific piece of code in Java to execute. The if keyword is always written in lowercase letters. If you write it in uppercase letters like If or IF, the compiler will generate an error. Let us test some conditions using the if statement and see how it works in Java.

```
public class JavaX {
   public static void main(String[] args) {
     if (300 > 30) {
        System.out.println("Yes, 300 is
greater than 30.");
     }
   }
}
```

```
Yes, 300 is greater than 30.
```

If you have a code that contains two variables, you can test them as well. I will use two variables a and b and include an if statement in the code to test the condition.

```
public class JavaX {
   public static void main(String[] args) {
     int a = 3000;
     int b = 3;
```

```
    if (a > b) {
        System.out.println("a appears to be
way greater than b");
    }
  }
}
```

```
a appears to be way greater than b
```

The else Statement

The above examples dealt with the situation in which conditions are always true. However, this is hardly the case in all situations. You may confront a situation in which a condition may turn out to be false when you execute it. That's the point we can use the else statement.

```
public class JavaX {
  public static void main(String[] args) {
    int time = 15;
    if (time < 16) {
        System.out.println("Have a good
morning. Be productive and creative.");
    } else {
        System.out.println("Good evening.
Sweet dreams! ");
    }
  }
}
```

```
Have a good morning. Be productive and
creative.
```

If I change the condition in the code, the display message will change. See the following example as to how it works.

```
public class JavaX {
  public static void main(String[] args) {
    int time = 15;
    if (time < 14) {
      System.out.println("Have a good
morning. Be productive and creative.");
    } else {
      System.out.println("Good evening.
Sweet dreams! ");
    }
  }
}
```

Good evening. Sweet dreams!

In the first piece of code, the condition is true as 16 is greater than 15. The less than condition is false, making the condition true. That's why we got the first message displayed on the screen. In the second piece of code, the 15 is greater than 14 so the condition is false. Here the else statement will get into action and display the second message on the screen.

The else if Statement

You can use the else if statement for specifying any new condition if a previous condition turns out to be false. The else if statement will be our third block of code. When the first two conditions turn out to be false, the third block of code, which is the else if statement, gets into action. In the following example, I will use the same code I used for the first two conditionals and add a third block of code to it. Let us see how it works.

```
public class JavaX {
```

```
    public static void main(String[] args) {
        int time = 15;
        if (time < 14) {
            System.out.println("Have a good
morning. Be productive and creative.");
        } else if (time < 20) {
            System.out.println("It is a bright
noon.");
        }
        else {
            System.out.println("Good evening.
Sweet dreams! ");
        }
    }
}
```

```
It is a bright noon.
```

Java Switch Statement

When there are multiple code blocks but you need to execute only one of them, you have to use the switch statement to execute the desired block of code. You can evaluate the switch statement only once. Each case in the block of code presents itself for comparison with the value of each expression. In case of a match, the targeted block of code is immediately executed. You may come other keywords like default and break. I will explain them later on. I will use the switch statement in the following code to see how it can be used to pick one of the several code lines in a lengthy and complex program. I will use a small program that indicates the weekdays and the related activities for each weekday.

```
    public class JavaX {
```

```java
public static void main(String[] args) {
    int tezday = 3;
    switch (tezday) {
      case 1:
        System.out.println("Monday is
blue.");
        break;
      case 2:
        System.out.println("Tuesday fires up
the momentum.");
        break;
      case 3:
        System.out.println("Wednesday brings
full speed to work.");
        break;
      case 4:
        System.out.println("Thursday keeps
up the momentum.");
        break;
      case 5:
        System.out.println("Friday finishes
key tasks and gets you ready to get
relaxed.");
        break;
      case 6:
        System.out.println("Saturday is
sleepy.");
        break;
      case 7:
        System.out.println("Sunday is all
about food.");
        break;
    }
  }
}
Wednesday brings full speed to work.
```

You might have noticed the break keyword in the code. When Java reaches the break keyword in the program, it breaks out of the block, stopping the execution of the code for a while. The case statement is put to test in the block. If there is no match, the compiler proceeds to the next statement. It keeps executing the code and stopping for a while to test until it finds a match. When the job is done, it is time to take a break. You don't need any more testing. A break statement saves the execution time because it tends to ignore the execution of the code inside the switch block.

The Default Keyword

Suppose the compiler has run through each case in the code and found no match. In this situation, we can use the default keyword to specify the block of code that must be executed if the compiler finds no match. I will use the same code example to explain how you can add the default keyword to the code.

```
public class JavaX {
  public static void main(String[] args) {
    int tezday = 10;
    switch (tezday) {
      case 1:
        System.out.println("Monday is
blue.");
        break;
      case 2:
        System.out.println("Tuesday fires up
the momentum.");
        break;
      case 3:
        System.out.println("Wednesday brings
full speed to work.");
```

```java
            break;
        case 4:
            System.out.println("Thursday keeps
up the momentum.");
            break;
        case 5:
            System.out.println("Friday finishes
key tasks and gets you ready to get
relaxed.");
            break;
        case 6:
            System.out.println("Saturday is
sleepy.");
            break;
        case 7:
            System.out.println("Sunday is all
about food ");
            break;
        default:
            System.out.println("I am planning a
vacation for the Weekend.");
    }
  }
}
```

I am planning a vacation for the Weekend.

Chapter Six

Java Loops

The while loop does not have a fixed number of steps that you need to execute. Therefore, you do not always need a counter in the code. The total number of repetitions of the while statement depend on how many times you evaluate the continuation condition to be true. A while statement does not need the initialization statement in the block of code or out of the statement. The while statement may replace the for statement in most of the cases. However, the major advantage of the for statement that keeps developers from quitting it is that it can encapsulate the initialization of the code. Also, the for statement offers the termination condition and counter modification. You can get all that in a single block, which makes the for statement superior to the while loop. However, each statement has its distinct advantages and disadvantages.

In programming, sometimes, you need repetitive steps that demand the same variables. To write the statement over and over again to get the job done would be painful. Loops make this job easy and fun.

Java loops tend to loop through blocks of code until the condition turns true. The code, in the below mentioned example, will repeatedly run until the variable in the code block is less than 7. Let us write the code and see how it works. I will explain the code after that.

```
public class JavaX {
   public static void main(String[] args) {
      int x = 0;
      while (x < 7) {
         System.out.println(x);
         x++;
      }
   }
}

0
1
2
3
4
5
6
```

The declaration as well as the initialization of the counter variable int x=0 exists out of the statement. However, the increment of the counter is executed in the code block. The repetition also starts here. Also, one major benefit of using the while loop is that the condition in the block of code is not quite necessary. The condition also is not mandatory at this point. You can replace it entirely with true. However, you need to make sure that you have included an exit condition in the block of code that will execute at one or the other point. Otherwise, the execution of the block of code is likely to end up in error. This particular condition should be replaced at the start of the code to prevent the execution of some useful logic where it must not be.

The most important thing to keep in mind is that you should increase the variable x or the loop will be infinite. It will never end and ultimately crash the program it is a part of.

The while statement works best when you are working with a specific resource that is never always online. Let us say you are using a remote database for your application that exists in an unstable network. The while statement helps you save your data over multiple timeouts until you succeed.

The do-while Loop

The do-while loop is no different from the while loop. The only difference is that the condition for continuation is generally evaluated in the former loop after the code block has been executed. This triggers the code block to be executed at least once unless the developer embeds the exit condition in the code. In most cases, the do-while and while loops can be easily and flawlessly interchanged. In most cases, you need a minimum change in the logic of the code block. Traversing the array and the printing of values of the elements may be written by using the do-while loop. There is no need to change the code.

The do-while loop statement works perfectly well when the code block needs to be executed at least once. Otherwise, you have to evaluate the condition at least once.

In the following example, I will use the do-while loop. The compiler will let the statement execute once even if the condition turns out to be false in the first run. Its reason is that the code block, which exists before the condition, is always tested.

```java
public class JavaX {
  public static void main(String[] args) {
    int x = 0;
    do {
      System.out.println(x);
      x++;
    }
    while (x < 7);
  }
}

0
1
2
3
4
5
6
```

For Loops

The for loop is highly recommended for the iteration of the objects such as lists and arrays that need to be counted. For example, traversing of an array and then printing the same can be done easily by the for loop.

```java
public class JavaX {
  public static void main(String... args) {
    int array[] = {50, 31, 12344, 42, 53};
```

```
for (int x = 0; x < array.length; ++x) {
System.out.println("This is Java array[" +
x + "] = " + array[x]);
 }
 }
 }
```

```
This is Java array[0] = 50
This is Java array[1] = 31
This is Java array[2] = 12344
This is Java array[3] = 42
This is Java array[4] = 53
```

When you are using the for loop, you need to know exactly how many times you need to loop through a specific block of code. In this kind of situation, the while loop does not work. The first statement in the code is executed once, right before the execution of the block of code. The second statement tends to define the specific condition for the execution of the block of code. The third statement is executed each time after the execution of the block of code. Let us see another example.

```
public class JavaX {
   public static void main(String[] args) {
     for (int x = 0; x < 7; x++) {
       System.out.println(x);
     }
   }
}
```

```
0
1
2
3
```

4
5
6

In the first statement, the variable is defined and set up before the start of the loop. In the second statement, the condition is defined so that the loop has something to understand and run. If the condition returns as true, the loop starts all over again. If the condition returns as false, the loop will reach its end. In the third statement, the variable's value increases each time the block of code inside the loop is executed.

By changing the condition, we can affect the output of the for loop. The following code will print the multiple of three.

```java
public class JavaX {
   public static void main(String[] args) {
      for (int x = 0; x <= 15; x = x + 3) {
         System.out.println(x);
      }
   }
}
```

0
3
6
9
12
15

The for-each Loop

The next loop I will explain is the for-each loop. The for-each loop is used exclusively to looping through different elements inside an array. In the following example, I will use an array of kitchen accessories and print all the elements using the for-each loop. See how it is different from the standard for loop. Please note down the difference in the code block as well.

```
public class JavaX {
  public static void main(String[] args) {
    String[] kitchen = {"spatula", "spoon",
"napkin", "ladle", "steak hammer"};
    for (String x : kitchen) {
      System.out.println(x);
    }
  }
}

spatula
spoon
napkin
ladle
steak hammer
```

Breaking Loops

In previous examples, I pointed out that you must use the break statement to exit a loop. You can use and manipulate the break statement in three ways.

1. The break statement is used to exit a loop. If a label accompanies the break statement, it will break the loop. This comes extremely handy when you are working with nested loops, because that's how you can break from the nested loops and not only the one that contains this statement.

2. The continue statement is used to skip any execution of code after it. It then move on to the next step.

3. The return statement is generally used for exiting a certain method so is the loop, the if statement, or the switch statement are inside the body of the method, you can use it to exit the loop. As per the best practices, the use of return statements for exiting a method must not be abused as they might risk the execution harder to follow up.

The break Statement

The break statement may only be used in switch, do-while, and while statements. You have seen how it can be used inside a code. You have seen what results it produces in a code. I have used it when I explained the switch statement. Now, I will demonstrate the use of the break statement in all the other types of loops. You can break out of the for loop, while loop, or do-while loop with the help of the break statement. However, you must control it by the exit condition otherwise you will not be able to execute a single step. In the next example, I will restrict the loop to some elements even if the loop traverses all the elements.

```
public class JavaX {
 public static final int thisarray[] = {5,
 1, 2, 3, 4};
 public static void main(String... args) {
 for (int x = 0; x < thisarray.length ; ++x)
 {
 if (x == 4) {
```

```
  System.out.println("You have reached the
end of the loop!");
 break;
 }
 System.out.println("the looped through
value: [" + x + "] = " + thisarray[x]);
 }
 }
}


the looped through value: [0] = 5
the looped through value: [1] = 1
the looped through value: [2] = 2
the looped through value: [3] = 3
You have reached the end of the loop!
```

If you are working with nested loop, you can use a label to decide which looping statement you can use to break out of the loop. In the following code, I will use three for loops nested well in the code block. I will exit the middle loop when the indexes become equal.

```
public class JavaX {
 public static final int thisarray[] = {5,
1, 4, 2, 3};
 public static void main(String... args) {
 for (int x = 0; x < 4; ++x) {
 TIM: for (int y = 0; y < 2; ++y) {
 for (int z = 0; z < 2; ++z) {
 System.out.println("(x variable, y
variable, z variable) = (" + x + "," + y +
"," + z + ")");
 if (x == y && y == z) {
 break TIM;
 }
 }
```

```
        }
      }
    }
  }
```

```
(x variable, y variable, z variable) =
(0,0,0)
(x variable, y variable, z variable) =
(1,0,0)
(x variable, y variable, z variable) =
(1,0,1)
(x variable, y variable, z variable) =
(1,1,0)
(x variable, y variable, z variable) =
(1,1,1)
(x variable, y variable, z variable) =
(2,0,0)
(x variable, y variable, z variable) =
(2,0,1)
(x variable, y variable, z variable) =
(2,1,0)
(x variable, y variable, z variable) =
(2,1,1)
(x variable, y variable, z variable) =
(3,0,0)
(x variable, y variable, z variable) =
(3,0,1)
(x variable, y variable, z variable) =
(3,1,0)
(x variable, y variable, z variable) =
(3,1,1)
```

The label that is used in the code is named as TIM. It tends to come before the for statement. The for statement is exited upon the fulfilment of the condition. It then follows the break statement.

Writing the name of labels in capital letters is considered the best practice in writing the code as it will avoid confusing labels with class or variables named when they are reading the code.

To make sure that this works, you may take a look inside the console to take a look that all the combinations of x, y, z are no longer printed. All the sets that start with 0 are automatically skipped.

The continue Statement

The continue statement does not necessarily break the loop. However, it can be used to skip different steps in line with the condition. Basically, it will stop the present step of the loop and then proceed to the next step. So that you can say that the statement goes on in the loop. This time I will traverse through the array but the only difference will be the addition of the continue statement.

```
public class JavaX {
 public static final int thisarray[] = {5,
1, 4, 2, 3};
 public static void main(String... args) {
 for (int x = 0; x < thisarray.length; ++x)
{
 if (x % 2 != 0) {
 continue;
 }
 System.out.println("the array [" + x + "] =
" + thisarray[x]);
 }
 }
}
```

```
the array [0] = 5
the array [2] = 4
the array [4] = 3
```

The above mentioned condition must be conditioned properly otherwise the loop will keep iterating endlessly and uselessly. The continue statement must be used with labels. Let us take apply similar example to nested for loops that have been used earlier on. However, this time when the z index comes equal to 1, you will see nothing printed on the screen.

```
public class JavaX {
 public static final int thisarray[] = {5,
1, 4, 2, 3};
 public static void main(String... args) {
 for (int x = 0; x < 3; ++x) {
 TIM:
 for (int y = 0; y < 3; ++y) {
 for (int z = 0; z < 3; ++z) {
 if (z == 1) {
 continue TIM;
 }
 System.out.println("(variable x, variable
y, variable z) = (" + x + "," + y + "," + z
+ ")");
 }
 }
 }
 }
}
```

```
(variable x, variable y, variable z) =
(0,0,0)
(variable x, variable y, variable z) =
(0,1,0)
```

```
(variable x, variable y, variable z) =
(0,2,0)
(variable x, variable y, variable z) =
(1,0,0)
(variable x, variable y, variable z) =
(1,1,0)
(variable x, variable y, variable z) =
(1,2,0)
(variable x, variable y, variable z) =
(2,0,0)
(variable x, variable y, variable z) =
(2,1,0)
(variable x, variable y, variable z) =
(2,2,0)
```

The return Statement

The return statement is easier to execute. You can use it to exit a method's execution. If a certain method returns a value, the return statement is usually accompanied in line with the value that is returned in the end. The return statement may be used to exit any statements that have been mentioned in the section. It represents a smarter way to shortcut the execution process as the execution halts for a while and the processing goes on from the point inside the code that is named as method. Now I will write a method that hunts down the first element in the array. The method will return the index or it will return -1.

```
public class JavaX {
 public static final int thisarray[] = {5,
 1, 4, 3, 2, 10, 12};
 public static void main(String... args) {
 int x = yeven(thisarray);
 if (x != -1) {
```

```
    System.out.println("The first even number
is as follows: " + x);
    }
}
public static int yeven(int ... thisarray)
{
for (int a = 0; a < thisarray.length; ++a)
{
if (thisarray[a] %2 == 0) {
return a;
}
}
return -1;
}
}
```

```
The first even number is as follows: 2
```

Now I will test the same code by replacing the for statement with the while statement and see how it works.

```
public class JavaX {
    public static final int thisarray[] = {5,
1, 4, 3, 2, 10, 12};
    public static void main(String... args) {
    int x = yeven(thisarray);
    if (x != -1) {
    System.out.println("The first even number
is as follows: " + x);
    }
}
public static int yeven(int ... thisarray)
{
    int a = 0; while (a < thisarray.length) {
    if (thisarray[a] %2 == 0) {
    return a;
```

```
    }
  ++a;
    }
  return -1;
    }
  }
```

```
The first even number is as follows: 2
```

You can use the return statement in any situation in which you want to terminate the execution of the loop in case a certain condition has been met.

Try-Catch Constructions

There is another method to control the flow of the code blocks. Try-catch statements are used for flow-control as an alternative to conditionals and loops. There is a general code block in the code for execution purposes. Then there is a declaration that may be thrown by code block. To handle the exception, there is another code block. Once you have caught the exception, you can execute the piece of code for treatment purposes. Then comes the clean-up code, which releases some resources or sets objects to null so they stay eligible for collection purposes. I will use the same array to build a try-catch construction.

```
public class JavaX {
public static final int thisarray[] = {5,
1, 4, 2, 3};
public static void main(String... args) {
try {
tezNoEven(thisarray);
```

```java
System.out.println("I have not found
anything, all is well!");
} catch (thisisanEvenException e) {
System.out.println(e.getTheMessage());
} finally {
System.out.println("The system is cleaning
up the thisarray.");
for (int z = 0; z < thisarray.length; ++z)
{
thisarray[z] = 0;
}
}
}
public static int tezNoEven(int...
thisarray) throws thisisanEvenException {
for (int z = 0; z < thisarray.length; ++z)
{
if (thisarray[z] % 2 == 0) {
throw new thisisanEvenException("I am not
expecting any even number at " + z);
}
}
return -1;
}
}
```

Chapter Seven

Java Methods

A method is a block of code that runs only when you call it. You can pass on information to methods. The information or data that you pass is known a parameters. Methods are used for performing a number of actions. They also are known as functions. Methods are brilliant because you can create them and reuse them after you define them once.

You must declare a method inside of a class. You must define it with the name of the method, properly followed by parentheses(). Java offers a bunch of pre-defined methods like system.out.println(). However, you also can create your methods for performing a set of actions.

```
public class JavaX {
   static void thisMeth() {
     System.out.println("The pirates have
plundered the ship!");
   }

   public static void main(String[] args) {
     thisMeth();
```

```
     }
   }
```

```
The pirates have plundered the ship!
```

In this example, the term thisMeth() is the name of the method. The keyword static means that this method belongs to JavaX class and not to any object of the JavaX class. The term void means that the method lacks a return value. I will explain more about return values in the later parts of the chapter. In the above mentioned example, I have made a method call, which, in turn, displayed the message that I had included in the message. The best thing about methods is that you can make multiple method calls once you have created them.

```
public class JavaX {
   static void thisMeth() {
      System.out.println("The pirates have
plundered the ship!");
   }

   public static void main(String[] args) {
      thisMeth();
      thisMeth();
      thisMeth();
   }
}
```

```
The pirates have plundered the ship!
The pirates have plundered the ship!
The pirates have plundered the ship!
```

Java Method Parameters & Arguments

You can pass on information to methods in the form of parameters. Parameters, inside a method, act as variables. Parameters are generally specified after the name of the method within the parentheses. You may add as many parameters to a method as you need. All you have to do is separate them by a comma. The following example has a method and parameters that pass on information to the method.

```java
public class JavaX {
  static void thisMeth(String name) {
    System.out.println(name + " is building
my house with the architect Rhodes");
  }

  public static void main(String[] args) {
    thisMeth("John");
    thisMeth("Seema");
    thisMeth("Kane");
  }
}

John is building my house with the architect
Rhodes
Seema is building my house with the
architect Rhodes
Kane is building my house with the architect
Rhodes
```

When you pass on a parameter to a method, it is known as argument. In the above method, name is parameter while Seema, Kane, and John are arguments.

Multiple Parameters

You have seen the use of one parameter in methods. In the next example, I will use more than one parameters to improve the usability of methods. I will explain the method to use as many parameters as you need in one method. This means that you can add as many information to a method as you can.

```
public class JavaX {
   static void thisMeth(String name, int age)
{
      System.out.println(name + " is building
my house with the architect Rhodes. He is "
+ age + ".");
   }

   public static void main(String[] args) {
      thisMeth("John", 45);
      thisMeth("Seema", 19);
      thisMeth("Kane", 22);
   }
}

John is building my house with the architect
Rhodes. He is 45.
Seema is building my house with the
architect Rhodes. He is 19.
Kane is building my house with the architect
Rhodes. He is 22.
```

When you are working with more than one parameter, the method call should contain the same number of arguments as the parameters. The arguments need to be passed in the perfect order.

Return Values

The void keyword in the code shows that the method must not necessarily return a value. if you want to get a value returned, you must use primitive data types like char and int instead of void. You also have to use the keyword return in the method.

```
public class JavaX {
  static int thisMeth(int a) {
    return 50 + a;
  }

  public static void main(String[] args) {
    System.out.println(thisMeth(5000));
  }
}

5050
```

The return keyword can work with more than one parameter. See the following example that has two parameters.

```
public class JavaX {
  static int thisMeth(int a, int b) {
    return b + a;
  }

  public static void main(String[] args) {
    System.out.println(thisMeth(5000, 50));
  }
}

5050
```

When you return a value through a method, you can channel it toward a variable and store it to use it later on in the program. The process is simple. All we need is a third variable for the code. In the following example, I will add a third variable in the code and send the returned result.

```
public class JavaX {
  static int thisMeth(int a, int b) {
    return b + a;
  }

  public static void main(String[] args) {
    int c = thisMeth(5000, 50);
    System.out.println(c);
  }
}
```

```
5050
```

Method Overloading

With the help of method overloading, multiple methods may take the same name with the help of different parameters. The following example has two methods that add different types of numbers.

```
public class JavaX {
  static int thisMethInt(int a, int b) {
    return a + b;
  }

  static double thisMethDouble(double a,
  double b) {
    return a + b;
  }
```

```
public static void main(String[] args) {
    int theNum1 = thisMethInt(80, 50);
    double theNum2 = thisMethDouble(6.3,
8.26);
    System.out.println("the int number : " +
theNum1);
    System.out.println("the double number: "
+ theNum2);
  }
}


the int number : 130
the double number: 14.559999999999999
```

Instead of defining the two methods that will ultimately do the same thing, you should overload one method. It will save space. In the following example, I will overload one method for the two types of numbers.

```
public class JavaX {
  static int thisMethplus(int a, int b) {
    return a + b;
  }

  static double thisMethplus(double a,
double b) {
    return a + b;
  }

  public static void main(String[] args) {
    int theNum1 = thisMethplus(80, 50);
    double theNum2 = thisMethplus(6.3,
8.26);
```

```
    System.out.println("the int number : " +
theNum1);
    System.out.println("the double number: "
+ theNum2);
  }
}
```

x

```
the int number : 130
the double number: 14.559999999999999
```

Scope

The variables in Java are only accessible in the region they are created in, which is called scope. The variables declared in a method can be located and traced after the line of code they are declared in.

```
public class JavaX {
   public static void main(String[] args) {

      int a = 100;

      System.out.println(a);
   }
}
```

```
100
```

Block of Scope

A block of code alludes to the code that exists between curly braces. The code can only access the variables that are declared in the blocks of code in between curly braces, which ultimately follows the line on which the programmer declares the variable.

```
public class JavaX {
  public static void main(String[] args) {

    {
      int a = 500;

      System.out.println(a);

    }

  }
}

500
```

Java Recursion

Recursion in Java is a technique to make a function call by itself. The technique offers a way to break down complicated problems into simple problems that are usually easier to solve. Recursion may get a lot tough to understand. However, the best way to find out how it works it to experiment with the same.

The addition of two numbers is easy but the addition of a range of different numbers is complicated. In the following example, I have used recursion to add a wide range of numbers by breaking them down into simple task of adding two numbers.

```
public class JavaX {
  public static void main(String[] args) {
    int theresult = summingup(20);
    System.out.println(theresult);
  }
  public static int summingup(int a) {
```

```
        if (a > 0) {
          return a + summingup(a - 1);
        } else {
          return 0;
        }
      }
    }

    210
```

Halting Condition

As loops run into one or another problems of becoming infinite loops, recursive functions have the same tendency of becoming infinite recursion. Infinite recursion happens when the function never stops making a call to itself. Every recursive function must have a halting condition, which is where your function will stop making a call to itself. In the past example, the halting condition occurred where the parameter became zero. In the next example, the function will add multiple numbers between the start and the end. The halting condition for the recursive function is when the end is never greater than the start.

```
public class JavaX {
  public static void main(String[] args) {
    int theresult = summingup(50, 100);
    System.out.println(theresult);
  }
  public static int summingup(int thestart,
int theend) {
    if (theend > thestart) {
      return theend + summingup(thestart,
theend - 1);
    } else {
```

```
        return theend;
    }
  }
}

3825
```

Advanced Method Concepts

There are a couple of more method concepts that you must take into consideration. The first is about the use of arrays in methods. You have learned how to integrate primitive data types in the code. Apart from the primitive data types, you can use arrays as well. You can use arrays as parameters. For that purpose, you need to use square brackets after the parameter's data type in the method's declaration. When you need to call this method, you must declare the array and then pass it on to an argument to your method.

You also can return an array from a method. To ensure the return in a method, you should add square brackets after the return type inside the declaration of methods. First of all, declare an array and then assign to it the result of the method.

```
package arraymethoddemo;

import java.util.Arrays;
class ThisClass{

public void printingtheFirstElement(int[]
x)
{
System.out.println("The first element in
the array will be " + x[0]);
```

```
}

public int[] returningtheArray()
{
int[] x = new int[3];
for (int y = 0; y < x.length; y++)
{
x[y] = y*2;
}
return x;
}


}

public class ArrayMethodDemo {
public static void main(String[] args) {

ThisClass amd = new ThisClass();

int[] ThisArray = {1, 2, 3, 4, 5};
amd.printingtheFirstElement(ThisArray);

int[] ThisArray2 = amd.returningtheArray();

System.out.println(Arrays.toString(ThisArray
2));

}
}

The first element in the array will be 1
[0, 2, 4]
```

I have included a couple of classes in the same file to keep it simple and easy for reading and practicing. There are two methods in the ThisClass. The first method is labeled as printingtheFirstElement().

This shows how to use an array in the form of a parameter. The second method returningtheArray() shows how you can return the array in the second phase. I then initialized the ThisClass object known as amd in the main() method. I then declared the array and also passed it on as argument to printingtheFirstElement() method. I also declared a second array inside the main() method and then assigned the result of returningtheArray() method to the same. Then I printed the contents.

This Keyword

The following example uses the this keyword to access the total number of classes.

```
public class ThisKeyword {
    // This is the Instance sum of variables
    int number = 100;

    ThisKeyword() {
        System.out.println("This is a
brilliant example program built around the
keyword this");
    }

    ThisKeyword(int number) {
        // I am invoking default constructor
in the following step
        this();

        // I am assigning a local variable
number to instance variable number
        this.number = number;
    }
```

```java
    public void greetings() {
        System.out.println("Hello, you are
welcome to the world of Java.");
    }

    public void printing() {
        // This is the total Local variable
number
        int number = 200;

        // I am now printing a local variable
        System.out.println("The total value of
the local variable number is as follows :
"+number);

        // I am now printing an instance
variable
        System.out.println("The total value of
the instance variable number is as follows :
"+this.number);

        // I am now invoking the greetings
method for this class
        this.greetings();
    }

    public static void main(String[] args) {
        // I am now instantiating a class
        ThisKeyword objectA = new
ThisKeyword();

        // I am now Invoking my print method
        objectA.printing();
```

```
        // I am now passing a new value to
number variable through the parametrized
constructors
        ThisKeyword objectB = new
ThisKeyword(50);

        // I will now invoke the print method
once again
        objectB.printing();
        // I am now passing a new value to
number variable through the parametrized
constructors
        ThisKeyword objectC = new
ThisKeyword(50000);

        // I will now invoke the print method
once again
        objectC.printing();
        // I am now passing a new value to
number variable
        ThisKeyword objectD = new
ThisKeyword(340000);

        // I will now invoke the print method
once again
        objectD.printing();
    }
}
```

This is a brilliant example program built around the keyword this

The total value of the local variable number is as follows : 200

The total value of the instance variable number is as follows : 100

Hello, you are welcome to the world of Java.

This is a brilliant example program built around the keyword this

The total value of the local variable number is as follows : 200

The total value of the instance variable number is as follows : 50

Hello, you are welcome to the world of Java.

This is a brilliant example program built around the keyword this

The total value of the local variable number is as follows : 200

The total value of the instance variable number is as follows : 50000

Hello, you are welcome to the world of Java.

This is a brilliant example program built around the keyword this

The total value of the local variable number is as follows : 200

The total value of the instance variable number is as follows : 340000

Hello, you are welcome to the world of Java.

Variable Arguments (var-args)

The Java Development Kit enables you to passing different number of arguments of similar types to a specific method. In the declaration of a method, you can specify its type followed by ellipsis(…). Just one variable-length may be specified in the method. The parameter must be the last of the parameters.

```java
public class VarargumentsDemonstration {

    public static void main(String args[]) {
        // I am now Calling the method with
the help of variable arguments
            printingMax(34, 355, 31, 22, 56.5);
        printingMax(new double[]{1, 2, 3});
    }

    public static void printingMax( double...
nums) {
        if (nums.length == 0) {
            System.out.println("There are no
argument passed");
            return;
        }

        double theresult = nums[0];

        for (int x = 1; x <  nums.length; x++)
        if (nums[x] >  theresult)
        theresult = nums[x];
        System.out.println("The maximum value
of the variable is " + theresult);
    }
}

The maximum value of the variable is 355.0
The maximum value of the variable is 3.0
```

Java Files

The Java.io package has all the classes you might need to execute input and output operations in Java. All the streams represent input source and the output destination as well. The stream inside the java.io package will support several data types like primitives, objects, and localized characters.

A stream may be defined as a data sequence. A stream generally is of two types like an InputStream and OutputStream. The first is used for reading data from a specific resource while the second is used for writing and feeding data to a specific destination. Java offers powerful support for I/O related files and networks.

Java Byte Streams can be used to process input and output of 8-bit size. Several classes are related to byte streams but the most used of them are FileOutputStream and FileInputStream. See the following example.

```java
import java.io.*;
public class CopyingtheFile {

    public static void main(String args[])
throws IOException {
        FileInputStream in = null;
        FileOutputStream out = null;

        try {
            in = new
FileInputStream("thisisinput.txt");
            out = new
FileOutputStream("thisisoutput.txt");

            int x;
            while ((x = in.read()) != -1) {
                out.write(x);
            }
        }finally {
```

```
        if (in != null) {
            in.close();
        }
        if (out != null) {
            out.close();
        }
    }
}
```

Character Streams

Java Byte Streams are usually used for performing input and output for the 8-bit bytes. On the other hand, Java Character streams may be used for performing the input and output of 16-bit Unicode. The most frequently used classes in Character streams are FileWriter and FileReader.

```
import java.io.*;
public class CopyingtheFile {

    public static void main(String args[])
    throws IOException {
        FileReader in = null;
        FileWriter out = null;

        try {
            in = new
FileReader("thisisinput.txt");
            out = new
FileWriter("thisisoutput.txt");

            int x;
            while ((x = in.read()) != -1) {
                out.write(x);
```

```
            }
        }finally {
            if (in != null) {
                in.close();
            }
            if (out != null) {
                out.close();
            }
        }
    }
}
```

This program will create an output file that will have the same content that the input file had.

Standard Streams

Programming languages provide support for standard I/O where user's program take the input from keyboard and then produce the output on the screen. If you are acquainted with C or C++ programming languages, you need to be aware of three standard devices - STDIN, STDERR, and STDOUT. Java provides three standard streams such as Standard Error, Standard Input, and Standard Output.

Standard Input is generally used for feeding data to the user's program. For this purpose, keyboard us used as the input stream. Standard output is used to process the output of data that is produced by a user's program. Usually programmers use a computer screen for the standard output stream. Standard Error is used to process the output error data that is produced by user's program. A computer screen is generally used for standard error stream and is represented as System.err.

```java
import java.io.*;
public class ReadingTheConsole {

    public static void main(String args[])
throws IOException {
        InputStreamReader cin = null;

        try {
            cin = new
InputStreamReader(System.in);
            System.out.println("Here you can
Enter the characters, enter 'q' for quitting
the program.");
            char x;
            do {
                x = (char) cin.read();
                System.out.print(x);
            } while(x != 'q');
        }finally {
            if (cin != null) {
                cin.close();
            }
        }
    }
}
```

Chapter Eight

Java Classes

OOP in Java stands for object oriented programming. Procedural programming in Java is about composing methods and procedures that will perform certain operations on your data. In contrast, object-oriented programming focuses on the creation of objects that contain methods and data. Object oriented programming carries multiple advantages over procedural programming. It is faster than procedural programming and is quite easier to execute.

Object oriented programming offers a clear structure for programs. It also helps keep Java code from repeating itself and cluttering the program. It makes your code easier to maintain, debug or modify. It also makes it possible for you to create reusable applications with less code and a shorter development time. Consequently, it will save you resources. The object oriented programming technique favors the DRY principle, known as Don't Repeat Yourself in full form. This principle focuses on cutting down on the repetition of code. You must slice out the codes that are common to your application, and then place them in a single place. From there you can take them and reuse them instead of repeating them.

Classes

Classes and objects are two parts of object oriented programming. A class is like a general template for objects and an object is like an instance of a single class. when you create individual objects, they will inherit the variables and different methods from the class.

Everything in Java is connected with objects or classes, and their methods or attributes. A leopard is an object and it has attributes like height, color, and gestures. It sits, eats, runs, and fights. Similarly, we give attributes to the objects in Java classes. In the following example, I will create an object from a class. I will use the keyword new along with the name of the object.

```
public class JavaX {
   int a = 50;

   public static void main(String[] args) {
      JavaX Obj1 = new JavaX();
      System.out.println(Obj1.a);
   }
}

50
```

You can create more than objects in a class. See the demonstration in the following example.

```
public class JavaX {
   int a = 50;
```

```
    public static void main(String[] args) {
        JavaX Obj1 = new JavaX();
        JavaX Obj2 = new JavaX();
        System.out.println(Obj1.a);
        System.out.println(Obj2.a);
    }
}

50
50
```

You can create an object and then access the same in another class. This more often is used for the better organization of classes. One class takes all the methods and attributes while the other class has one main method. You need to remember that the name of the Java file you are saving your code in must match the name of the class.

Java Class Attributes

You can access the attributes of a class by creating a class object and also by using the dot syntax. The following example will create object of a class. I will use the a attribute on the object to print the value.

```
public class JavaX {
    int a = 50;

    public static void main(String[] args) {
        JavaX Obj1 = new JavaX();
        System.out.println(Obj1.a);
    }
}
50
```

Modifying Attributes

Changing values of attributes becomes imminent at times. You need to replace the old values with new values. You can modify the attributes of classes by the following method.

```java
public class JavaX {
   int a;

   public static void main(String[] args) {
      JavaX Obj1 = new JavaX();
      Obj1.a = 400;
      System.out.println(Obj1.a);
   }
}
```

```
400
```

Even if the initial value of the attribute a is something like 20, you can modify it. I will change 20 to 400 inside the class without removing the first value. That's called the process of modifying attributes in Java classes.

```java
public class JavaX {
   int a = 20;

   public static void main(String[] args) {
      JavaX Obj1 = new JavaX();
      Obj1.a = 400;
      System.out.println(Obj1.a);
   }
}
```

```
400
```

If you are writing a large-scale code and don't want other programmers to change the value, you can block modification by declaring its attribute final. You will see an error in return. See the following example.

```
public class JavaX {
    final int a;

    public static void main(String[] args) {
        JavaX Obj1 = new JavaX();
        Obj1.a = 400;
        System.out.println(Obj1.a);
    }
}

JavaX.java:6: error: cannot assign a value
to final variable a
        Obj1.a = 400;
              ^
1 error
```

Multiple Objects

If you create more than one object of a single class, you can change the values of the attributes in one object without affecting the attribute values in another class.

```
public class JavaX {
    int a = 50;

    public static void main(String[] args) {
        JavaX Obj1 = new JavaX();
        JavaX Obj2 = new JavaX();
        Obj2.a = 555;
        System.out.println(Obj1.a);
```

```
      System.out.println(Obj2.a);
   }
}

50
555
```

You can add as many attributes as you like.

```java
public class JavaX {
   String name = "John";
   String profession = "doctor";
   int theage = 32;

   public static void main(String[] args) {
      JavaX Obj1 = new JavaX();
      System.out.println("The name is " +
Obj1.name + ".");
      System.out.println("I am working as a "
+ Obj1.profession + ".");
      System.out.println("My age is " +
Obj1.theage + ".");
   }
}

The name is John.
I am working as a doctor.
My age is 32.
```

Class Methods

You have already learned how you can create methods and how you can use them. Java methods are always parts of classes. They are declared inside the classes and they are used to perform several actions. See the following example in which I will create a method inside the JavaX class.

```java
public class JavaX {
  static void thisMeth() {
    System.out.println("This is Java
Class!");
  }

  public static void main(String[] args) {
    thisMeth();
  }
}
```

```
This is Java Class!
```

Static vs Non-Static Attributes

Java programs have static or public attributes as well as methods. The following example will demonstrate the functioning of static or public methods.

```java
public class JavaX {
  // This is the Static method
  static void thisIsStaticMethod() {
    System.out.println("You can call Static
methods without the creation of objects.");
  }

  // This is the Public method
  public void thisIsPublicMethod() {
    System.out.println("You must call public
methods by creating objects.");
  }
```

```
// This is the Main method
public static void main(String[] args) {
   thisIsStaticMethod(); // This is our
Call for the static method

   JavaX Obj1 = new JavaX(); // Here I will
create an object of
   Obj1.thisIsPublicMethod(); // This step
is used to Call the public method
   }
}
```

You can call Static methods without the creation of objects

You must call public methods by creating objects

You can access Java methods with the help of objects. In the following object, I will create a bike class. Then I will call a couple of methods on the object and kick off the program.

```
// I am Creating here the JavaX class
public class JavaX {

   // It is time to create the fullspeed()
method
   public void topThrottle() {
      System.out.println("The racer is running
the bike at full throttle!");
   }

   // In the following step, I will create
the speed() method and then I will add to it
a parameter
   public void bikespeed(int maximumSpeed) {
```

```
        System.out.println("The Maximum speed of
    the bike is " + maximumSpeed + "mph.");
        }

        // Inside JavaX class, I will call on the
    methods on the bike1 object
        public static void main(String[] args) {
            JavaX bike1 = new JavaX();        // It is
    time to create the bike1 object
            bike1.topThrottle();        // I am now
    calling the topThrottle() method
            bike1.bikespeed(500);            // I am
    now calling the bikespeed() method
        }
    }

    The racer is running the bike at full
    throttle!
    The Maximum speed of the bike is 500mph.
```

In the above example, I have created the JavaX class with the help of the class keyword. Then I created the topThrottle() method and the bikespeed() method inside the JavaX class. The bikespeed() method takes the int parameter that is designated as maximumSpeed. One thing still missing is an object that will use the JavaX class and the relevant methods. Then I used the main() method that is a Java built-in method. It runs your program and all the codes inside are executed one by one.

The new keyword in the program is used to create a new object namely bike1. Once that object has been created, I used the topThrottle() and bikespeed() methods on the newly created object bike1. The program is then run by using the object name bike1. If you notice, you will find a dot(.) after the object's name bike1. The dot is then followed by the name of the two methods that I have already created. The dot(.) is the way to access the attributes and methods for the object. When you want to call a method in Java, you should add parentheses () and a semicolon(). A class needs to carry a matching filename or it will not function well.

Multiple Objects

In the following example, I will create more than one objects to see how it is done and how it works. I will add two more bikes to the class as objects. Each of them has different maximum speed levels however all of them are running at full throttle. I will not make any changes to the code but add more code at the end to create different objects.

```java
// I am Creating here the JavaX class
public class JavaX {

  // It is time to creating the fullspeed()
method
   public void topThrottle() {
     System.out.println("The racer is running
the bike at full throttle!");
   }

   // In the following step, I will create
the speed() method and then I will add to it
a parameter
   public void bikespeed(int maximumSpeed) {
     System.out.println("The Maximum speed of
the bike is " + maximumSpeed + "mph.");
   }
```

```
// Inside JavaX class, I will call on the
methods on the bike1 object
  public static void main(String[] args) {
    JavaX bike1 = new JavaX();      // It is
time to create the bike1 object
    bike1.topThrottle();      // I am now
calling the topThrottle() method
    bike1.bikespeed(500);        // I am
now calling the bikespeed() method
    JavaX bike2 = new JavaX();      // It is
time to create the bike1 object
    bike2.topThrottle();      // I am now
calling the topThrottle() method
    bike2.bikespeed(300);        // I am
now calling the bikespeed() method
    JavaX bike3 = new JavaX();      // It is
time to create the bike1 object
    bike3.topThrottle();      // I am now
calling the topThrottle() method
    bike3.bikespeed(400);        // I am
now calling the bikespeed() method
  }
}
```

The racer is running the bike at full
throttle!
The Maximum speed of the bike is 500mph.
The racer is running the bike at full
throttle!
The Maximum speed of the bike is 300mph.
The racer is running the bike at full
throttle!
The Maximum speed of the bike is 400mph.

Multiple Classes

It is the best practice to create an object and then access the same in another class. The only most important thing is that you should keep the name of the java file in accordance with the name of the class. As there will be two classes, I will create two java files bearing the class names inside the same directory. The following example will explain the code and the method to create multiple classes.

```java
// I am Creating here the JavaX class
public class JavaX {

  // It is time to creating the fullspeed()
method
    public void topThrottle() {
      System.out.println("The racer is running
the bike at full throttle!");
    }

  // In the following step, I will create
the speed() method and then I will add to it
a parameter
    public void bikespeed(int maximumSpeed) {
      System.out.println("The Maximum speed of
the bike is " + maximumSpeed + "mph.");
    }
}
```

The above-mentioned section will go to the file name JavaX. This is the main class and it needs a separate file to be saved in. The following section will be saved in the second file named after the name of the class. See below which part will take a separate file.

```
Class Bike{
  // Inside JavaX class, I will call on the
methods on the bike1 object
  public static void main(String[] args) {
    JavaX bike1 = new JavaX();        // It is
time to create the bike1 object
    bike1.topThrottle();        // I am now
calling the topThrottle() method
    bike1.bikespeed(500);            // I am
now calling the bikespeed() method
    JavaX bike2 = new JavaX();        // It is
time to create the bike1 object
    bike2.topThrottle();        // I am now
calling the topThrottle() method
    bike2.bikespeed(300);            // I am
now calling the bikespeed() method
    JavaX bike3 = new JavaX();        // It is
time to create the bike1 object
    bike3.topThrottle();        // I am now
calling the topThrottle() method
    bike3.bikespeed(400);            // I am
now calling the bikespeed() method
  }
}
```

As the name of the class is Bike, the name of the file will be Bike as well.

Java Constructors

A Java constructor is used to initialize objects. The java constructor may be called when you create a class object. You can also use it to set up the initial values for the attributes of an object.

```
// I am creating the JavaX class
```

130

```java
public class JavaX {
  int a;

  // In the following line of code, I will
  create a class constructor for JavaX class
  public JavaX() {
    a = 5;
  }

  public static void main(String[] args) {
    JavaX Obj1 = new JavaX();
    System.out.println(Obj1.a);
  }
}

5
```

You must note that the Java constructor needs to match the name of the class. Also, you cannot add a return type in this code. You can only call the constructor when you create an object. All the Java classes need to have constructors by default. If you do not create one, Java will do that for you. However, in that situation, you will not be able to set up the initial values for the object's attributes.

Java constructors can take certain parameters that are used to initialize attributes. In the following example, I will add a parameter to the Java constructor. Inside the constructor, I will pass parameter to the constructor. See the following example to understand how to do that.

```java
public class JavaX {
  int a;
```

```
public JavaX(int b) {
  a = b;
}

public static void main(String[] args) {
  JavaX Obj1 = new JavaX(50);
  System.out.println(Obj1.a);
}
}
```

50

You can add to the code as many parameters as you need to.

```
public class JavaX {
  int mYear;
  String mName;

  public JavaX(int year, String name) {
    mYear = year;
    mName = name;
  }

  public static void main(String[] args) {
    JavaX bike1 = new JavaX(2020, "BMW");
    System.out.println(bike1.mYear + " " +
bike1.mName + " are the make year and model
of my bike.");
    JavaX bike2 = new JavaX(2015, "Harley
Davidson");
    System.out.println(bike2.mYear + " " +
bike2.mName + " is worth 500k.");
    JavaX bike3 = new JavaX(2014, "'s
Suzuki");
```

```
    System.out.println(bike3.mYear + "" +
bike3.mName + " costs a fortune but worth
investment.");
    }
}
```

```
2020 BMW are the make year and model of my
bike.
2015 Harley Davidson is worth 500k.
2014's Suzuki costs a fortune but worth
investment.
```

Java Inner Classes

You can nest classes in Java. This means you can put one class into another. The main goal of nesting classes is to group the classes that must be placed together. This makes the code readable. See the following example. When you have to access the inner class, you can create one object in the outer class and one object in the inner class.

```
class TheOuterClass {
   int a = 100;

   class TheInnerClass {
     int b = 5000;
   }
}

public class Main {
   public static void main(String[] args) {
     TheOuterClass myOuter1 = new
TheOuterClass();
     TheOuterClass.TheInnerClass myInner1 =
myOuter1.new TheInnerClass();
```

```
      System.out.println(myInner1.b +
myOuter1.a);
   }
}
```

5100

Unlike the regular class, the inner class can be protected or private.
If you don't need outside objects for accessing the inner class and
declaring classes as private.

```
class TheOuterClass {
   int a = 100;

   private class TheInnerClass {
      int b = 50;
   }
}

public class Main {
   public static void main(String[] args) {
      TheOuterClass Outer1 = new
TheOuterClass();
      TheOuterClass.TheInnerClass Inner1 =
Outer1.new TheInnerClass();
      System.out.println(Inner1.b + Outer1.a);
   }
}

Main.java:12: error:
TheOuterClass.TheInnerClass has private
access in TheOuterClass
      TheOuterClass.TheInnerClass Inner1 =
Outer1.new TheInnerClass();
                    ^
```

```
Main.java:12: error:
TheOuterClass.TheInnerClass has private
access in TheOuterClass
    TheOuterClass.TheInnerClass Inner1 =
Outer1.new TheInnerClass();

    ^

2 errors
```

You will see an error because you cannot access a private class from the outside class.

Static Inner Class

Your inner class may be static. This means that it can accessed even if you don't create an object of outer class.

```
class TheOuterClass {
  int a = 100;

  static class TheInnerClass {
    int b = 50;
  }
}

public class Main {
  public static void main(String[] args) {
    TheOuterClass.TheInnerClass Inner1 = new
TheOuterClass.TheInnerClass();
    System.out.println(Inner1.b);
  }
}

50
```

Accessing Outer Class From Inner Class

The biggest advantage of the inner classes is that they tend to access the attributes and methods of outer classes.

```
class TheOuterClass {
  int a = 100;

  class TheInnerClass {
    public int TheInnerMethod() {
      return a;
    }
  }
}

public class Main {
  public static void main(String[] args) {
    TheOuterClass Outer1 = new
TheOuterClass();
    TheOuterClass.TheInnerClass Inner1 =
Outer1.new TheInnerClass();

System.out.println(Inner1.TheInnerMethod());
  }
}

100
```

Chapter Nine

Modifiers, User Input, Interfaces

You might have noticed a heavy use of the word 'public' in the codes. The public keyword is labeled as access modifier. It means that you can use it to set up the access level for your classes, methods, attributes and constructors. There are different types of modifiers in Java; one is called access modifiers and the other one is called non-access modifiers. The access modifiers tend to control the access level while the non-access modifiers need not control the access level. Instead, it provides some other kind of functionality.

For classes, you can use default or public modifier. When you add public to a class, you label the class as literally public. Anyone can access the class, edit it or modify it. The default modifier for a class makes the class accessible only by other classes inside a package. You can set the modifier to default when you don't want to specify a modifier.

```
public class JavaX {
  public static void main(String[] args) {
    System.out.println("The public modifier
makes this class accessible to anyone.");
```

```
        }
    }
```

To use the default method, all you need to do is remove the public keyword from the above code like this:

```
class JavaX {
    public static void main(String[] args) {
        System.out.println("The public modifier
makes this class accessible to anyone.");
    }
}
```

When you are dealing with method, attributes, and constructors, you can use the following modifiers.

```
public class JavaX {
    public String name = "David";
    public String profession = "Coach";
    public String contact = "DDavid@dye.com";
    public int age = 48;
}
```

Now I will set the attributes to private, which means that now the attributes will only be accessible inside the declared class. See the following example.

```
public class JavaX {
    private String name = "David";
    private String profession = "Coach";
    private String contact = "DDavid@dye.com";
    private int age = 48;

    public static void main(String[] args) {
        JavaX Obj1 = new JavaX();
```

```
    System.out.println("The name is: " +
Obj1.name + ".");
    System.out.println("My profession is " +
Obj1.profession + ".");
    System.out.println("My contact Email is:
" + Obj1.contact);
    System.out.println("My age is " +
Obj1.age + ".");
  }
}
```

```
The name is: David.
My profession is Coach.
My contact Email is: DDavid@dye.com
My age is 48.
```

If we set the attributes to default, the code will only be accessible to those that exist in the same package. You can use the default method when you are no longer in need of a modifier. I will now remove the public and private keywords, which will revert the code to default settings.

```
class JavaX {
  String name = "David";
  String profession = "Coach";
  String contact = "DDavid@dye.com";
  int age = 48;

  public static void main(String[] args) {
    JavaX Obj1 = new JavaX();
    System.out.println("The name is: " +
Obj1.name + ".");
    System.out.println("My profession is " +
Obj1.profession + ".");
```

```
    System.out.println("My contact Email is:
" + Obj1.contact);
    System.out.println("My age is " +
Obj1.age + ".");
  }
}
```

You can set up the code to protected, which means that the code will be accessible only inside the same package and in the subclasses only.

```
class JavaX {
  protected String name = "David";
  protected String profession = "Coach";
  protected String contact =
"DDavid@dye.com";
  protected int age = 48;
}
```

Non-Access Modifiers

Java offers some non-access modifiers for classes. The final modifier will keep the class from getting inherited by other classes. I will explain the process of inheritance in the following chapters. You can use the final modifier when you don't want to let the overriding of existing values. You will see an error if you attempt to override the code.

```
public class JavaX {
  final int a = 100;
  final double b = 3.14;

  public static void main(String[] args) {
    JavaX Obj1 = new JavaX();
```

```
    Obj1.x = 50; // The override will
generate error
    Obj1.b = 25; // The override will
generate error
    System.out.println(Obj1.a);
  }
}


JavaX.java:7: error: cannot find symbol
    Obj1.x = 50; // The override will
generate error
         ^
  symbol:   variable x
  location: variable Obj1 of type JavaX
JavaX.java:8: error: cannot assign a value
to final variable b
    Obj1.b = 25; // The override will
generate error
         ^
2 errors
```

Static Method

There is another method namely static. This means that you can access it without the creation of a class object. This is contrary to the keyword public.

```
public class JavaX {
  // This is the static method
  static void StatMethod() {
    System.out.println("You can call Static
methods even if you don't create objects");
  }

  // This is the Public method
  public void PubMethod() {
```

```
        System.out.println("You can call public
methods by creating certain objects.");
    }

    // This is the Main method
    public static void main(String[] args) {
        StatMethod(); // I am making a Call for
the static method

        JavaX Obj1 = new JavaX(); // I will now
create an object
        Obj1.PubMethod(); // I am now Calling
public method
    }
}
```

You can call Static methods even if you don't create objects

You can call public methods by creating certain objects.

Abstract

The abstract method is connected with the abstract class. It lacks a body. The subclass provides the body for the class.

```
    // This is the abstract class
    abstract class JavaX {
        public String name = "David";
        public String profession = "Coach";
        public String contact = "DDavid@dye.com";
        public int age = 48;
    }

    // Subclass (you will inherit it from the
JavaX class)
    class Coach extends JavaX {
```

```
public int trainingCourse = 2015;
public void coaching() {
  System.out.println("I coach for full
year under my booster coaching session.");
  }
}
```

The following code will take a separate Java file because it has a separate class.

```
class Secondclass {
  public static void main(String[] args) {
    Coach Obj1 = new Coach();

    System.out.println("Name: " +
Obj1.name);
    System.out.println("Profession: " +
Obj1.profession);
    System.out.println("Training course: " +
Obj1.trainingCourse);
    Obj1.coaching();
  }
}
```

The abstract keyword is a non-access modifier. You can use if for methods and classes. An abstract class is restricted and cannot be used to create objects. You must inherit it from another class to access it. An abstract method only belongs to an abstract class. It lacks a body, which is provided by the subclass. Abstract classes entertain regular methods as well as abstract methods.

```
// This is an example of the Abstract class
abstract class AnimalKingdom {
  // The following Abstract method lacks a
have a body
```

```
    public abstract void animalSounds();
    // The following method is a Regular
method
    public void sleepmode() {
      System.out.println("SnoooooooooZzz");
    }
}

// This is a Subclass that has been
inherited from AnimalKingdom
class Leopard extends AnimalKingdom {
    public void animalSounds() {
      // I have provided the body of
animalSounds() in the following method
      System.out.println("The leopard says:
meow meow.");
    }
}

class Main {
    public static void main(String[] args) {
      Leopard leopard1 = new Leopard(); // I
am creating a leopard object
      leopard1.animalSounds();
      leopard1.sleepmode();
    }
}

The leopard says: meow meow.
SnoooooooooZzz
```

You can use abstract classes when you need high security. Using abstract classes, you can hide some of the details and only show the most important details in a program. You can achieve abstraction with the help of interfaces.

Encapsulation

You can only access private variables inside the same class. An outside class can never access it. However, there is a way out. You can access them if you provide the public set and get methods. The get method will return the value of the variable and the set method will set up its value. The syntax starts with set or get keywords. Then you have to put in the name of the variable. The first letter of the variable should be in upper case.

The get method will return the variable's value while the set method will take parameters and assign them to the same variable that gets handled in the first step. In the code, there is a this keyword. The this keyword refers to the current object that is under work.

```
public class JavaX {
  public static void main(String[] args) {
    Man Obj1 = new Man();
    Obj1.name = "Johnny Boy";
    System.out.println(Obj1.name);
  }
}
```

The following code takes a second file because it has a separate class name.

```
public class Man {
  private String name;

  public String gettheName() {
    return name;
  }

  public void settheName(String newName) {
```

```
        this.name = newName;
      }
   }
JavaX.java:3: error: cannot find symbol
      Man Obj1 = new Man();
        ^
   symbol:    class Man
   location: class JavaX
JavaX.java:3: error: cannot find symbol
      Man Obj1 = new Man();
                       ^
   symbol:    class Man
   location: class JavaX
2 errors
```

Now I will use the getName() and setName() methods to update the variables. Now the methods will have access to the variables and there will be no error on your screen.

```
public class JavaX {
   public static void main(String[] args) {
      Man Obj1 = new Man();
      Obj1.setName = "Johnny Boy";
      System.out.println(Obj1.getName);
   }
}

public class Man {
   private String name;

   public String gettheName() {
      return name;
   }

   public void setName(String newName) {
      this.name = newName;
```

```
          }
     }
```

Encapsulation offers improved control of the methods and attributes of classes. You can make the attributes of the class read-only or write-only if you use only the set method. You can change one section of the code and still it will not affect the other sections of the code. The process will also help improve the security.

Java Enums

A Java Enum is a special Java class that represents a specific group of constants. These constants cannot be changed and are called final variables. To create an enum, you can use the enum keyword instead of an interface or class, and then separate all the constants with the help of a comma. All must be in uppercase letters. Enum is the short form of enumerations, its meaning is specially listed and you can integrate an enum inside the Java class.

```
public class Main {
  enum TezLevel {
    LOW,
    MEDIUM,
    HIGH
  }

  public static void main(String[] args) {
    TezLevel Var1 = TezLevel.MEDIUM;
    System.out.println(Var1);
  }
}

MEDIUM
```

You can add enum inside a switch statement as well. See the following example for reference. Inside the switch statement, the enums are used for checking corresponding values.

```
enum TezLevel {
  LOW,
  MEDIUM,
  HIGH
}

public class Main {
  public static void main(String[] args) {
    TezLevel Var1 = TezLevel.MEDIUM;

    switch(Var1) {
      case LOW:
        System.out.println("You are at the
Lowest level in the code.");
        break;
      case MEDIUM:
        System.out.println("You are at the
Medium level in the code.");
        break;
      case HIGH:
        System.out.println("You have reached
the Highest level now.");
        break;
    }
  }
}
```

```
You are at the Medium level in the code.
```

You can change the level and get different results by the following method.

```
enum TezLevel {
  LOW,
  MEDIUM,
  HIGH
}

public class Main {
  public static void main(String[] args) {
    TezLevel Var1 = TezLevel.HIGH;

    switch(Var1) {
      case LOW:
        System.out.println("You are at the
Lowest level in the code.");
        break;
      case MEDIUM:
        System.out.println("You are at the
Medium level in the code.");
        break;
      case HIGH:
        System.out.println("You have reached
the Highest level now.");
        break;
    }
  }
}
```

```
You have reached the Highest level now.
```

Building Loops

You can build a loop through the enum type. The loop will return a full array of the enum constants. The method comes handy when you are looking forward to loop through all the enum constants.

```
enum TezLevel {
```

```
    LOW,
    MEDIUM,
    HIGH
}

public class Main {
  public static void main(String[] args) {
    for (TezLevel Var1 : TezLevel.values())
{
      System.out.println(Var1);
    }
  }
}

LOW
MEDIUM
HIGH
```

An enum, like a class, carries attributes and it can also have methods. The only difference is that the enum constants are final, public, and static. You cannot override them. They cannot help you create objects. Also, you cannot extend them to other classes as well. However, they can implement interfaces. The best way to use them is for values like colors, months, years, and weekdays, which do not change in any case.

Java User Input

You can use the Scanner class in Java to receive user input. The class can be obtained from java.util package. If you want to use the class, you have to create an object and then apply the available methods of Scanner class. There are multiple methods for the

Scanner class. In the following example, I will use the nextLine()
method that is specially used to read different types of strings.

```java
import java.util.Scanner; // Here I am
importing Scanner class from the package

class Main {
  public static void main(String[] args) {
    Scanner ThisObj = new
Scanner(System.in);
    String myuserName;

    // Please Enter the username and after
that press Enter
    System.out.println("I need you to Enter
the username we have allotted you.");
    myuserName = ThisObj.nextLine();

    System.out.println("The Username is as
follows: " + myuserName);
  }
}
```

The methods differ with respect to the type of input. In the next
example, I will use other methods to read a value from users.

```java
import java.util.Scanner;

class Main {
  public static void main(String[] args) {
    Scanner Obj1 = new Scanner(System.in);

    System.out.println("I want you to Enter
your name, your age and current salary:");

    // This is the String input
```

```
String tezname = Obj1.nextLine();

// This is the Numerical input
int tezage = Obj1.nextInt();
double tezsalary = Obj1.nextDouble();

// This will be the Output input by the
user
System.out.println("The Name of the
user: " + tezname);
System.out.println("The Age of the user:
" + tezage);
System.out.println("The Salary of the
user: " + tezsalary);
    }
}
```

Java Interfaces

The top way to find out abstraction inside Java is done with the help of interfaces. A Java interface is an abstract class that you can use to group up the methods with the help of empty bodies. If you want to access interface methods, you need to implement the interfaces by another class using the implements keyword. You can provide the body of interface method by using the implement class.

```
interface AnimalKingdom {
  public void animalSounds(); // This is the
interface method and it does not have body
  public void sleepmode(); // This is the
interface method and it does not have a body
  }

class Leopard implements AnimalKingdom {
  public void animalSounds() {
```

```java
      System.out.println("The leopard says:
meow meow");
    }
    public void sleepmode() {
      System.out.println("Zzz");
    }
}

class JavaX {
    public static void main(String[] args) {
      Leopard Pig1 = new Leopard();
      Pig1.animalSounds();
      Pig1.sleepmode();
    }
}

The leopard says: meow meow
Zzz
```

Like the abstract classes, the interfaces have no part in creating objects. The methods interfaces lack a body. The implement class provides the body to the interfaces. You will need to override every other method when you set up and implement an interface. They are public and abstract, and their attributes are final, public or static. You must use interfaces for achieving high level security. You can use them to hide some details and show the important details of objects.

```java
interface Interface1 {
  public void ThisMethod(); // This is the
interface method
}

interface Interface2 {
```

```java
    public void TheOtherMethod(); // This is
the second interface method
}

// the DemoClass named as "implements" are
known as Interface1 and Interface2
class DemonstrationClass implements
Interface1, Interface2 {
  public void ThisMethod() {
    System.out.println("Here is some text
for review..");
  }
  public void TheOtherMethod() {
    System.out.println("Here is some more
text for testing...");
  }
}

class JavaX {
  public static void main(String[] args) {
    DemonstrationClass Obj1 = new
DemonstrationClass();
    Obj1.ThisMethod();
    Obj1.TheOtherMethod();
  }
}
Here is some text for review..
Here is some more text for testing...
```

Chapter Ten

Java Object Oriented

In Java, you can inherit attributes and different methods from multiple classes. The concept of inheritance is divided into two categories such as superclass and subclass. The keyword that is used for inheritance is extends.

A class in Java can either be package-private or public. We have used the public classes for examples until now. Public means that the class may be accessed by any of the classes that exist in the program. On the other hand, package-private means that the class is only accessible to the other classes inside the same package. There may be more than one packages in one Java application. Package-private is the default access level. If you do not add any access modifier, it means that the class is highly package private. After you have declared class' access level, you need to type in the class keyword to indicate that you are declaring a class.

You have seen that I enclosed the contents of classes inside a pair of curly braces that follow the name of the class. The contents of a class carry constructors, interfaces, fields, methods, and other classes.

Inheritance

Inheritance is a key concept in object-oriented programming. It allows you to create a new class from an already created class so that you can reuse the existing code to develop another program or application. All classes in Java are primarily inherited from a pre-written base class. It is referred to as an object class. It consists of several pre-written methods that you can use when you work with classes. One such method is known as the toString() method. This method returns the string that represents an object. I will use the same in the next few examples.

Suppose we are working on a reading app which offers two membership programs like normal and VIP. Here is the code.

The following code will demonstrate how to create inheritance in Java. You the extends keyword will help inherit the methods.

```java
class Mathematics {
    int c;

    public void adding(int a, int b) {
        c = a + b;
        System.out.println("The total sum of
    our given numbers:"+c);
    }

    public void SubtractingNum(int a, int b)
    {
        c = a - b;
```

```java
        System.out.println("The final
difference between these numbers is as
follows:"+c);
    }
}

public class My_Mathematics extends
Mathematics {
    public void multiplying(int a, int b) {
        c = a * b;
        System.out.println("The final product
of our given numbers is:"+c);
    }

    public static void main(String args[]) {
        int x = 30, y = 30;
        My_Mathematics demo = new
My_Mathematics();
        demo.adding(x, y);
        demo.SubtractingNum(x, y);
        demo.multiplying(x, y);
    }
}
```

```
The total sum of our given numbers:60
The final difference between these numbers
is as follows:0
The final product of our given numbers
is:900
```

Now I will add another method to divide the numbers. See how to add it and apply it to the class.

```java
class Mathematics {
    int c;
```

```java
    public void adding(int a, int b) {
        c = a + b;
        System.out.println("The total sum of
our given numbers:"+c);
    }

    public void SubtractingNum(int a, int b)
{
        c = a - b;
        System.out.println("The final
difference between these numbers is as
follows:"+c);
    }
    public void Dividing(int a, int b) {
        c = a / b;
        System.out.println("The final division
between these numbers is as follows:"+c);
    }
}

public class My_Mathematics extends
Mathematics {
    public void multiplying(int a, int b) {
        c = a * b;
        System.out.println("The final product
of our given numbers is:"+c);
    }

    public static void main(String args[]) {
        int x = 30, y = 30;
        My_Mathematics demo = new
My_Mathematics();
        demo.adding(x, y);
        demo.SubtractingNum(x, y);
        demo.multiplying(x, y);
        demo.Dividing(x, y);
```

```
    }
}
```

```
The total sum of our given numbers:60
The final difference between these numbers
is as follows:0
The final product of our given numbers
is:900
The final division between these numbers is
as follows:1
```

In the inherited class, I will add the option of modulus to explain how it extends to the main class.

```
class Mathematics {
    int c;

    public void adding(int a, int b) {
        c = a + b;
        System.out.println("The total sum of
our given numbers:"+c);
    }

    public void SubtractingNum(int a, int b)
{
        c = a - b;
        System.out.println("The final
difference between these numbers is as
follows:"+c);
    }
    public void Dividing(int a, int b) {
        c = a / b;
        System.out.println("The final division
between these numbers is as follows:"+c);
    }
}
```

```java
public class My_Mathematics extends
Mathematics {
   public void multiplying(int a, int b) {
      c = a * b;
      System.out.println("The final product
of our given numbers is:"+c);
   }
   public void modulus(int a, int b) {
      c = a % b;
      System.out.println("The final modulus
of our given numbers is:"+c);
   }

   public static void main(String args[]) {
      int x = 30, y = 30;
      My_Mathematics demo = new
My_Mathematics();
      demo.adding(x, y);
      demo.SubtractingNum(x, y);
      demo.multiplying(x, y);
      demo.Dividing(x, y);
      demo.modulus(x, y);
   }
}
```

The total sum of our given numbers:60
The final difference between these numbers
is as follows:0
The final product of our given numbers
is:900
The final division between these numbers is
as follows:1
The final modulus of our given numbers is:0

In this program, when I create an object to the My_Mathematics class, the superclass also has a copy of the same. This is why you can access the members of the superclass by using the object of subclass. The superclass reference variable holds the subclass object. A subclass usually inherits all members like methods, fields, and nested classes from the superclass. The constructors are usually not members therefore they are not inherited by the subclasses. However, the constructor of superclass may be invoked from subclass.

The super keyword is like the this keyword. You can use it to differentiate between the members of superclass. You also can use it to invoke superclass constructor from the subclass. If a class inherits properties of another class and if superclass members carry the same names as the subclass, you can use super keyword to differentiate between variables in the following way.

```
super.method()
super.variable
```

In the next program, I will demonstrate the use of super keyword. There will be two classes with one method. There will be a variable as well that has different values. I will invoke the method of the two classes and then print the values of different variables of the two classes.

```
class SupClass {
    int number = 20;

    // I am displaying the methods of
superclass
```

161

```java
    public void displaying() {
        System.out.println("You are viewing
the display method of the superclass");
    }
}

public class SubClass extends SupClass {
    int number = 10;

    // I am now displaying the method of sub
class
    public void displaying() {
        System.out.println("You are viewing
the display method of the subclass");
    }

    public void thisMethod() {
        // I am now instantiating the subclass
        SubClass sub = new SubClass();

        // I am now Invoking displaying()
method for the sub class
        sub.displaying();

        // I am now Invoking the displaying()
method for the superclass
        super.displaying();

        // I am now printing the value of the
variable number of the subclass
        System.out.println("This is the value
of a variable named number in the sub
class:"+ sub.number);

        // Now I am printing value of the
variable number of the superclass
```

```
    System.out.println("The value of
variable namely number in the super class
is:"+ super.number);
    }

    public static void main(String args[]) {
        SubClass obj1 = new SubClass();
        obj1.thisMethod();
    }
}
```

```
You are viewing the display method of the
subclass
You are viewing the display method of the
superclass
This is the value of a variable named number
in the sub class:10
The value of variable namely number in the
super class is:20
```

Superclass Constructor

If a Java class inherits properties of another class, the subclass will require the default constructor of superclass. If you need to call the parameterized constructor of superclass, the use of the super keyword will be different. Here is the demonstration.

```
super(values);
```

The program in the section demonstrates the use of the super keyword for invoking parameterized constructor of superclass. I will add to the program a superclass and subclass. The superclass has a parameterized constructor that will take integer value. I will

163

use the super keyword for invoking this constructor inside superclass.

```
class SupClass {
    int theage;

    SupClass(int theage) {
        this.theage = theage;
    }

    public void gettheAge() {
        System.out.println("The final value of
variable theage inside the SupClass is: "
+theage);
    }
}

public class SubClass extends SupClass {
    SubClass(int theage) {
        super(theage);
    }

    public static void main(String argued[])
{
        SubClass s = new SubClass(24);
        s.gettheAge();
    }
}
```

```
The final value of variable theage inside
the SupClass is: 24
```

The subclasses in program inherit all the properties of superclass except the private properties of superclass.

```
class AnimalKingdom {
```

```
}

class MammalFamily extends AnimalKingdom {
}

class ReptileFamily extends AnimalKingdom {
}

public class DogFamily extends MammalFamily
{

    public static void main(String args[]) {
        AnimalKingdom a = new AnimalKingdom();
        MammalFamily m = new MammalFamily();
        DogFamily d = new DogFamily();

        System.out.println(m instanceof
AnimalKingdom);
        System.out.println(d instanceof
MammalFamily);
        System.out.println(d instanceof
AnimalKingdom);
    }
}

true
true
true
```

The implements keyword forms the IS-A relationship. The implements keyword is used inside classes for inheriting properties of interfaces. Classes do not extend these interfaces. Let us use the instanceof operator for checking whether Mammal family belongs to animal kingdom and dog also is of animal kingdom. This operator works perfectly well.

```
interface AnimalKingdom{}
class MammalFamily implements
AnimalKingdom{}

public class DogFamily extends MammalFamily
{

    public static void main(String args[]) {
        MammalFamily m = new MammalFamily();
        DogFamily d = new DogFamily();

        System.out.println(m instanceof
AnimalKingdom);
        System.out.println(d instanceof
MammalFamily);
        System.out.println(d instanceof
AnimalKingdom);
    }
}

true
true
true
```

If a class inherits method from superclass, the method that is not marked as final is likely to be overridden. There is a positive angle to this development. It provides you the ability to define a particular behavior that's belongs to the subclass type. This means that a subclass will implement the parent class method on the basis of the requirement. In object-oriented programming, overriding means overriding the total functionality of a specific method that already exists.

```
class AnimalKingdom {
```

```java
    public void moveon() {
        System.out.println("All the animals in
the kingdom can move.");
    }
}

class LeopardFamily extends AnimalKingdom {
    public void moveon() {
        System.out.println("Leopards have
tremendous capability to walk and run
wildly.");
    }
}

public class TestLeopard {

    public static void main(String args[]) {
        AnimalKingdom x = new AnimalKingdom();
// This is the AnimalKingdom reference and
its related object
        AnimalKingdom y = new LeopardFamily();
// This is the AnimalKingdom reference but
is specific to Leopard object

        x.moveon();    // This line will run
method in the AnimalKingdom class
        y.moveon();    // This will run method
in LeopardFamily class
    }
}
```

All the animals in the kingdom can move.
Leopards have tremendous capability to walk
and run wildly.

Let us make the program more complex by adding more instances for the object. I will add more methods to make the leopard more interactive and lively.

```
class AnimalKingdom {
    public void moveon() {
        System.out.println("All the animals in
the kingdom can move.");
    }
}

class LeopardFamily extends AnimalKingdom {
    public void moveon() {
        System.out.println("Leopards have
tremendous capability to walk and run
wildly.");
    }
    public void running() {
        System.out.println("Leopard is running
wildly in the jungle.");
    }
}

public class TestLeopard {

    public static void main(String args[]) {
        AnimalKingdom x = new AnimalKingdom();
// This is the AnimalKingdom reference and
its related object
        AnimalKingdom y = new LeopardFamily();
// This is the AnimalKingdom reference but
is specific to Leopard object

        x.moveon();    // This line will run
method in the AnimalKingdom class
```

```
        y.moveon();    // This will run method
in LeopardFamily class
        y.running();
    }
}

TestLeopard.java:24: error: cannot find
symbol
        y.running();
          ^
    symbol:    method running()
    location: variable y of type AnimalKingdom
1 error
```

Has it produced an unexpected result? I think you were not expecting an error in the end. The compile time error popped up on your screen because the y's reference type AnimalKingdom lacked a method by the name of running.

When you are overriding methods, there are some rules that you need to follow. The first rule is that the list of argument should be the same as of the overridden method. The second rule is that the return type must be the same of a subtype of return type, and is declared in the method that is overridden in the superclass.

You can only override the instance method if subclass inherits them. You cannot override a method that has already been declared or a method that is declared as static. However, you can re-declare it.

If you cannot inherit a method, you cannot override it as well. A subclass that exists in the same package as the superclass instance may override a superclass method that you have not declared as final or private.

A subclass that exists in a different package can override the non-final methods that have either been protected or declared public.

Overriding methods have the power to throw away uncheck exceptions. However, the overriding method must not throw checked exceptions that are broader than those that the overridden method has declared.

```
class AnimalKingdom {
   public void moveon() {
       System.out.println("All the animals in
the kingdom can move.");
   }
}

class LeopardFamily extends AnimalKingdom {
   public void moveon() {
       System.out.println("Leopards have
tremendous capability to walk and run
wildly.");
   }
}

public class TestLeopard {

   public static void main(String args[]) {
       AnimalKingdom x = new AnimalKingdom();
// This is the AnimalKingdom reference and
its related object
```

```
        x.moveon();   // This line will run
   method in the AnimalKingdom class

    }
}
```

All the animals in the kingdom can move.

Polymorphism

Polymorphism is the ability of a particular object to take up different forms. The most common polymorphism happens in object oriented programming when a particular parent class reference refers to an object of the child class. Any particular Java object that passes multiple IS-A test is considered as polymorphic. All Java objects are considered polymorphic since any of them will pass IS-A test for its own type.

With the help of a reference variable, you can access an object. The reference variable may be reassigned to different other objects that are not considered as final. The reference type determines the particular methods that it may invoke about the object. A reference variable refers to an object of any subtype of the declared type. You can declare a reference variable as an interface type.

A Buffalo class can take inheritances as Animal, Buffalo, Object, Dinner, Victim, Vegetarian, etc. In this situation, we may say that the Buffalo class is polymorphic.

In the next example, I will explain how overriding behavior in Java lets you take advantage of this specific trait of polymorphism while designing the classes.

In the following example, I will show how an overridden method stays hidden in parent classes. It is never invoked unless the child class deploys the super keyword in the overriding method.

```java
public class PublicEmployee {
    private String ename;
    private String eaddress;
    private int enumber;
    private int esalary;

    public PublicEmployee(String ename,
String eaddress, int enumber, int esalary) {
        System.out.println("I am in the
process of constructing a public Employee");
        this.ename = ename;
        this.eaddress = eaddress;
        this.enumber = enumber;
        this.esalary = esalary;
    }

    public void ThisIsmailCheck() {
        System.out.println("I have to mail a
check to " + this.ename + " " +
this.eaddress);
    }

    public String theString() {
        return ename + " " + eaddress + " " +
enumber + " " + esalary;
    }

    public String getename() {
        return ename;
    }

    public String geteaddress() {
```

172

```
        return eaddress;
    }

    public void seteaddress(String
neweaddress) {
        eaddress = neweaddress;
    }

    public int getenumber() {
        return enumber;
    }
    public int getesalary() {
        return esalary;
    }
}
```

Error: Main method not found in class PublicEmployee, please define the main method as:

```
    public static void main(String[] args)
or a JavaFX application class must extend
javafx.application.Application
```

The result is an error.

Chapter Eleven

Java Date & Time

The date class in Java tends to support two constructors. The first is Date() which initializes an object that has the current data and time. The second is the Date(long millisec) constructor, which accepts an argument equal to the total number of milliseconds that have elapsed since 1970.

There are different method for Java Date & Time feature. The first method is Boolean after (Date date), which returns true if the Date object contains a date that is specified by date. Otherwise, it returns as false. The second method is known as boolean before(Date date). It returns true if invoking the Date object will contain a specified date or it will return as false. The third method is Object clone() which duplicates the Date object.

Getting the current date and time is an easy method. The simple method toString() is used to print the current date and time. The method is as under:

```
import java.util.Date;
public class TheDateDemonstration {
```

```
    public static void main(String args[]) {
        // Here I will instantiate the Date
object
        Date date = new Date();

        // Here I will display the time and
date by using the toString() method
        System.out.println(date.toString());
    }
}
```

Thu May 13 09:31:53 UTC 2021

There are three ways to compare the dates in Java. The first is to use the getTime() method to get the total number of milliseconds that have elapsed since 1970 for objects. You can then compare the two values. The second method is to use the before(), equals() and after() methods. You also can deploy compareTo() method. This is defined by Comparable interface and then implemented by Date.

You can format the date in Java using SimpleDateFormat feature. It is a solid class to format and efficiently parse dates. The SimpleDateFormat class allows you to take a start by choosing defined patterns for the date-time formatting.

```
    import java.util.*;
    import java.text.*;

    public class DateDemonstration {

        public static void main(String args[]) {
            Date dNow = new Date( );
            SimpleDateFormat ft =
```

175

```
      new SimpleDateFormat ("E yyyy.MM.dd
'at' hh:mm:ss a zzz");

      System.out.println("Here is the
Current Date: " + ft.format(dNow));
   }
}


Here is the Current Date: Thu 2021.05.20 at
09:40:17 AM UTC
```

You also can format dates by using printf method. In this method, you use a two-letter format that starts with t. Here is the demonstration of the code.

```
import java.util.Date;
public class DateDemonstration {

   public static void main(String args[]) {
      // In this step, I will instantiate
the Date object
      Date date = new Date();

      // At this step, I will display the
time and date
      String string = String.format("Here is
the Current Date & Time : %tc", date );

      System.out.printf(string);
   }
}


Here is the Current Date & Time : Thu May 20
09:43:28 UTC 2021
```

Of course, you don't have the time to feed in the date multiple times to format each part of the program. That's why a format string will indicate the argument's index that should be formatted. The index needs to immediately follow % and it should be terminated by $.

```java
import java.util.Date;
public class DateDemonstration {

    public static void main(String args[]) {
        // Here I will Instantiate the Date object
        Date date = new Date();

        // Here I will display time and date of the program
        System.out.printf("%1$s %2$tB %2$td, %2$tY", "Due date:", date);
    }
}
```

```
Due date: May 20, 2021
```

If you don't want use this format, you can alternatively use the <flag. It indicates that you should use the same argument in preceding format.

```java
import java.util.Date;
public class DateDemonstration {

    public static void main(String args[]) {
        // Here I will Instantiate the Date object
        Date date = new Date();
```

```
        // Here I will display time and date
of the program
        System.out.printf("%s %tB %<td, %<tY",
"This is the final due date:", date);
    }
}
```

This is the final due date: May 20, 2021

Parsing Strings

The solid class SimpleDateFormat carries some additional methods as well. One of the most popular methods is parse(). This method attempts to parse a specific string according to the format stored in the SimpleDateFormat objects.

```
import java.util.*;
import java.text.*;

public class DateDemonstrations {

    public static void main(String args[]) {
        SimpleDateFormat ft = new
SimpleDateFormat ("yyyy-MM-dd");
        String Theinput = args.length == 0 ?
"The date 1818-11-11" : args[0];

        System.out.print(Theinput + " Will
parse as follows: ");
        Date t;
        try {
            t = ft.parse(Theinput);
            System.out.println(t);
        }catch (ParseException e) {
```

```
        System.out.println("Unparseable
using " + ft);
        }
    }
}
```

The date 1818-11-11 Will parse as follows:
Unparseable using
java.text.SimpleDateFormat@f67a0200

Sleep Feature

You can add the sleep feature to the code for any period from one millisecond to the overall life of the operating system I will push the following program to sleep. See how it is done. From the difference in the output's time and date, you will realize that the program had been sleeping for 9 seconds.

```
import java.util.*;
public class TheSleepDemonstration {

    public static void main(String args[]) {
        try {
            System.out.println(new Date( ) +
"\n");
            Thread.sleep(5*180*10);
            System.out.println(new Date( ) +
"\n");
        }catch (Exception e) {
            System.out.println("This is an
exception!");
        }
    }
}
```

Thu May 20 10:01:59 UTC 2021

Thu May 20 10:02:08 UTC 2021

Elapsed Time

You also can measure the elapsed time. You may feel the need to measure different points in time in the form of milliseconds.

```java
import java.util.*;
public class DifferenceDemonstration {

    public static void main(String args[]) {
        try {
            long thestart =
System.currentTimeMillis( );
            System.out.println(new Date( ) +
"\n");

            Thread.sleep(5*180*10);
            System.out.println(new Date( ) +
"\n");

            long theend =
System.currentTimeMillis( );
            long thedifference = theend -
thestart;
            System.out.println("The total
difference of time is as follows: " +
thedifference);
        }catch (Exception e) {
            System.out.println("Here is an
exception!");
        }
    }
}
```

```
Thu May 20 10:08:36 UTC 2021

Thu May 20 10:08:45 UTC 2021

Difference is : 9028
```

If you take a look at the Georgian Calendar, you will find out that it is a solid implementation of Calendar class. It implements the Gregorian Calendar that you use every day. The getInstance() method will return the Gregorian Calendar. It will be initialized with date and time in its default time zone. There will be two fields known as AD and BC. They will represent two eras by Gregorian Calendar.

```java
import java.util.*;
public class
TheGregorianCalendarDemonstration {

    public static void main(String args[]) {
        String months[] = {"January",
"February", "March", "April", "May", "June",
"July", "August", "September",
        "October", "November", "December"};

        int theYear;
        // I will now create the Gregorian
calendar
        // That will have the present date and
time in its
        // default locale as well as timezone.

        GregorianCalendar gregocalendar = new
GregorianCalendar();
```

```
        // Here I will display the current
time and date info.
        System.out.print("Here is the current
date: ");

System.out.print(months[gregocalendar.get(Ca
lendar.MONTH)]);
        System.out.print(" " +
gregocalendar.get(Calendar.DATE) + " ");
        System.out.println(theYear =
gregocalendar.get(Calendar.YEAR));
        System.out.print("Here is the current
time: ");

System.out.print(gregocalendar.get(Calendar.
HOUR) + ":");

System.out.print(gregocalendar.get(Calendar.
MINUTE) + ":");

System.out.println(gregocalendar.get(Calenda
r.SECOND));

        // Test if the current year is a leap
year
        if(gregocalendar.isLeapYear(theYear))
{
            System.out.println("This present
year is the leap year on Gregorian
Calendar");
        }else {
            System.out.println("The present
year is not the leap year on Gregorian
Calendar.");
        }
    }
```

```
    }
```

```
    Here is the current date: May 21 2021
    Here is the current time: 2:27:29
```

The present year is not the leap year on Gregorian Calendar.

Java RegEx

Java has the java.util.regex package to match different types of patterns with the help of regular expressions. Java regular expressions are easy to learn. A regular expression is like a special sequence of characters that will help you match a set of strings with the help of a specialized syntax held in a specific pattern. You can use them to search, then edit, and also exploit data.

The java.util.regex has three main classes. The first is the pattern class. An object in the Pattern class offers no public constructors. For creating a pattern, you should invoke one of the public static compile() methods, which will return the Pattern object. These specific methods tend to accept regular expression as first argument.

The matcher object is like an engine that will interpret the pattern and perform match operations against input strings. Like Pattern class, Matcher does not define the public constructors. You can obtain the Matcher by using the matcher() method on Pattern object. A PatternSyntaxException is like an unchecked exception that will point out error in the syntax in the form of a regular expression pattern.

Capturing groups are the best ways to treat different characters in the form of a single unit. You can create them by setting up the characters in the form of groups inside parentheses. The following example will show how to track a digit string from a alphanumeric string.

```java
import java.util.regex.Matcher;
import java.util.regex.Pattern;

public class TheRegexMatch {

    public static void main( String args[] )
{
        // Here you will see the String that
is to be scanned to track the pattern.
        String tezline = "You placed this
order for QT3000! OK?";
        String tezpattern = "(.*)(\\d+)(.*)";

        // I am creating a specific Pattern
object
        Pattern r =
Pattern.compile(tezpattern);

        // Here I will create a matcher
object.
        Matcher m = r.matcher(tezline);
        if (m.find( )) {
            System.out.println("The Found value
is as follows: " + m.group(0) );
            System.out.println("The Found value
is as follows: " + m.group(1) );
            System.out.println("The Found value
is as follows: " + m.group(2) );
        }else {
```

```
            System.out.println("I have found NO
    MATCH at the moment.");
            }
        }
    }
```

The Found value is as follows: You placed this order for QT3000! OK?

The Found value is as follows: You placed this order for QT300

The Found value is as follows: 0

RegEx Syntax

The following is given different regular expression metacharacters that Java entertains.

1. The subexpression ^ matches start of lines.

2. The subexpression $ matches end of lines.

3. The subexpression [...] matches a single character that exists inside the brackets.

4. The subexpression [^...] matches a single character but not inside the brackets.

5. The subexpression \A shows the start of a string.

6. The subexpression \z shows the end of string.

7. The subexpression \Z shows end of string except the allowable last line terminator.

8. The subexpression re* will match 0 or more occurrences than that of preceding expression.

9. The subexpression re+ matches 1 or more than 1 of the preceding thing.

10. The subexpression re? matches 0 or 1 occurrence of previous expressions.

Start and End Methods

The following example will count the total number of times that the word peacock is seen in the string that is meant for input.

```java
import java.util.regex.Matcher;
import java.util.regex.Pattern;

public class RegexMatching {

    private static final String REGEXM =
"\\bcat\\b";
    private static final String INPUTM = "cat
cat cat catie cat";

    public static void main( String args[] )
{
        Pattern p = Pattern.compile(REGEX);
        Matcher m = p.matcher(INPUT);    // I
will now get matcher object
        int countingit = 0;

        while(m.find()) {
            countingit++;
            System.out.println("Here is the top
Match number "+countingit);
```

186

```java
        System.out.println("Here is the
starting point(): "+m.start());
        System.out.println("Here is the
ending point(): "+m.end());
    }
  }
}
```

Chapter Twelve

Java Generics

J ava Generic methods and classes tend to enable programmers to specify a set of methods or a set of related methods with one declaration of class. Java generic provides compile-time type safety that will allow programmers to detect the invalid types at the time of compilation. By using Java Generic concept, I will write a generic method to sort out an array of different objects and then invoke a generic method with the help of Double arrays, Integer arrays, and String arrays.

Generic Methods

You may write one single method declaration that will be called with different types of arguments. Based on argument types passed to generic method, the Java compiler will handle each method appropriately. Here are the rules for defining Generic Methods.

1. All of the declarations of generic methods must have a type parameter section delimited by the angle brackets that will precede the method's return type.

2. Each type parameter contains multiple comma-separated parameters . A type parameter that also is known as the type variable is a sort of identifier that will specify the generic type name.

3. The type parameters may be used for the declaration of the return type and act as placeholders for the arguments that have been passed on to generic methods.

4. A generic method is declared like any other method. The parameters may represent the reference types only.

```
public class GenericMethodTesting {
    // This is a generic method printingArray
    public static < E > void printingArray(
E[] inputArray ) {
        // I will display the array elements
        for(E element : inputArray) {
            System.out.printf("%s ", element);
        }
        System.out.println();
    }

    public static void main(String args[]) {
        // I will Create a number of arrays
for Integer, Double and Character
        Integer[] integerArray = { 1, 2, 3, 4,
5, 6, 7, 9 };
        Double[] doublesArray = { 1.1, 2.2,
3.3, 4.4 };
        Character[] characterArray = { 'H',
'E', 'L', 'L', 'O' };
```

```
        System.out.println("The Array namely
integerArray contains:");
        printingArray(integerArray);    // This
will pass on the Integer array

        System.out.println("\nThe Array namely
doublesArray contains:");
        printingArray(doublesArray);    // This
will pass on the Double array

        System.out.println("\nThe Array
characterArray contains:");
        printingArray(characterArray);    //
This will pass on the Character array
    }
}

The Array namely integerArray contains:
1 2 3 4 5 6 7 9

The Array namely doublesArray contains:
1.1 2.2 3.3 4.4

The Array characterArray contains:
H E L L O
```

Bonded Type Parameters

There may be some times when you will need to restrict different types that must be passed to the type parameter. A method that will operate on the numbers might want to accept a couple of the subclasses. You need to list the name of the type parameter to declare a bonded type parameter. Then you will have to follow it up by the upper bound and extends keyword.

```java
public class MaxTesting {
    // This will determine the largest of the
    three Comparable obj

    public static <T extends Comparable<T>> T
    maximum(T a, T b, T c) {
        T maximum = a;    // This step will
    assume that the a variable is the largest

        if(b.compareTo(maximum) > 0) {
            maximum = b;    // This will assume
    that b is the largest
        }

        if(c.compareTo(maximum) > 0) {
            maximum = c;    // This assumes that
    c is the largest
        }
        return maximum;    // This code will
    return the largest object in the code
    }

    public static void main(String args[]) {
        System.out.printf("The Maximum value
    of %d, %d and %d is %d\n\n",
            30, 40, 50, maximum( 30, 40, 50 ));

        System.out.printf("The Maximum value
    of %.1f,%.1f and %.1f is %.1f\n\n",
            60.6, 80.8, 70.7, maximum( 60.6,
    80.8, 70.7 ));

        System.out.printf("The Maximum value
    of %s, %s and %s is %s\n","melon",
            "guava", "strawberry",
    maximum("melon", "guava", "strawberry"));
```

```
        }
    }
```

```
The Maximum value of 30, 40 and 50 is 50

The Maximum value of 60.6,80.8 and 70.7 is
80.8
```

The Maximum value of melon, guava and strawberry is strawberry

Generic Classes

A generic class declaration is like a non-generic class declaration except that its name contains a type parameter. The type parameter section of this generic class has multiple type parameters separated with the help of commas. These classes are labeled as parameterized classes because they accept multiple parameters.

```java
public class Boxing<T> {
    private T a;

    public void adding(T a) {
        this.a = a;
    }

    public T get() {
        return a;
    }

    public static void main(String[] args) {
        Boxing<Integer> integerBox = new
Boxing<Integer>();
        Boxing<String> stringBox = new
Boxing<String>();
```

```
      integerBox.adding(new Integer(100));
      stringBox.adding(new String("I am
learning Java programming."));

      System.out.printf("The final Integer
Value is as follows:%d\n\n",
integerBox.get());
      System.out.printf("The final String
Value is as follows :%s\n",
stringBox.get());
   }
}
The final Integer Value is as follows:100
```

The final String Value is as follows :I am learning Java programming.

Conclusion

Now you have made it to the end of the book, it is recommended that you practice as much as you can to understand this language better. The next step is to understand how you can use the codes in your programs. Based on the knowledge you have gained through this book, you can study advanced code samples on the internet and customize them to learn more.

Coding is tricky and hard grasp until you start practicing it yourself. It is a tough job until you build your own programs. I have started the book from the basics. You can capitalize on the basic knowledge once you gain mastery over the codes.

Java is the present and the future as well. It is not going to lose its immense popularity any time soon. Therefore, learning Java can be a highly profitable skill.

References

Java - Loop control. (n.d.).
https://www.tutorialspoint.com/java/java_loop_control.htm

Java - Numbers class. (n.d.). RxJS, ggplot2, Python Data
Persistence, Caffe2, PyBrain, Python Data Access, H2O,
Colab, Theano, Flutter, KNime, Mean.js, Weka, Solidity.
https://www.tutorialspoint.com/java/java_numbers.htm

Java - Polymorphism. (n.d.). RxJS, ggplot2, Python Data
Persistence, Caffe2, PyBrain, Python Data Access, H2O,
Colab, Theano, Flutter, KNime, Mean.js, Weka, Solidity.
https://www.tutorialspoint.com/java/java_polymorphism.ht
m

Java classes and objects. (n.d.). W3Schools Online Web Tutorials.
https://www.w3schools.com/java/java_classes.asp

Java HashMap. (n.d.). W3Schools Online Web Tutorials.
https://www.w3schools.com/java/java_hashmap.asp

Java interface. (n.d.).
https://www.w3schools.com/java/java_interface.asp

www.ingramcontent.com/pod-product-compliance
Lightning Source LLC
Chambersburg PA
CBHW061021220326
41597CB00016BB/1799